GW01003787

PAST LIVES
and
Present Relationships

PAST LIVES
and
Present Relationships

John Van Auken

INNER VISION
Publishing Company
Box 1117, Virginia Beach, Virginia 23451
Box 3367, Anaheim, CA 92803
(804) 425-2245

Dedicated to
Doris Ann Dean
For her sacrifice in helping me write this book.

This book is published by
Inner Vision Publishing Co.,
Box 1117, Virginia Beach, VA 23451
Box 3367, Anaheim, CA 92801
It is printed in the United States of America.

First Printing -- June 1985
Second Printing -- December 1986
Third Printing -- September 1987

ISBN 0-917483-01-4

CONTENTS

FOREWORD

PART ONE: A Distant Past

Chapter One

REINCARNATION & OUR
FORGOTTEN LIVES 1

Chapter Two

REINCARNATION & OUR
PRESENT RELATIONSHIPS 23

Chapter Three

EXAMPLES OF PAST LIVES
AND PRESENT RELATIONSHIPS 38

Chapter Four

THE LIVES OF LELA:
One Soul's Journey 47

PART TWO: The Present and Future

Chapter Five

HOW TO REMEMBER YOUR PAST LIVES .. 76

Chapter Six
STARTING WHERE YOU ARE:
A Practical Approach Toward
Working with Your Present Life
and Relationships 94

APPENDIX

Edgar Cayce 107

Reincarnation & Christianity 111

Books for Further Study 117

FOREWORD

There was a time when I felt reincarnation was just not possible. I certainly didn't feel like I had been alive before, and I knew very few people who did. Those who did always seemed a bit kooky to me. Nevertheless, I continued to consider the possibility that reincarnation could be occurring. I did this for two reasons. First, as much as I knew in my heart that all men were created equal, I saw no evidence of that around me. We all seemed to be born with distinct advantages and disadvantages. Why one child was born crippled and another whole was a question that plagued me. Secondly, there seemed to be little justice in the world. Reward did not always reflect effort or worthiness. Sometimes, even evil seemed to overcome good, which I knew in my heart was not the ultimate truth. I knew there simply had to be more to the story of life than I had been told. For these reasons I kept an open mind about reincarnation.

In this book, I have attempted to show why I now believe, even know, that reincarnation does indeed occur and that the story of life is much greater than we presently perceive. The horizons of birth and death are not the beginning and the end. Neither is a heaven or a hell the ultimate dwelling place for us.

PART ONE

THE DISTANT PAST

CHAPTER ONE
REINCARNATION &
OUR FORGOTTEN LIVES

The idea that you and I have reincarnated is some-what of a misconception. The "you" and "I" that we consider to be our normal, everyday selves has actually *not* reincarnated. Our conscious minds, personalities and physical bodies are, for the most part, fresh and new. Very few of us are born with the sophistication of a person who has lived many lifetimes and even fewer possess any memory of past lives. Our normal, every-day selves are alive for the first time, perhaps for the only time. We have not reincarnated.

However, there is an *inner* part of us that *has* been alive before. This part of us has incarnated in the Earth's dimension many times.

Perhaps the use of this metaphor will help to illus-trate. Our present life is like a new flower in a new meadow. In a real sense, this flower is alive for the first time. However, its life neither began in this meadow nor in this season. Its present life came here on unseen breezes from a distant flower in a distant meadow, and all the characteristics and experiences of that former flower (as well as all the flowers that preceded it) are having a significant effect on the present flower. In fact, what seems to be a new flower is actually the latest appearance of a life that has existed for ages, appearing for a time only to disappear and then re-appear again. From seed to plant to flower to seed again, this life has been carried on the winds of destiny and desire from the very beginning.

Like the flower, within each of us is the essence of our being. This essential part of us has been alive from the beginning and will live long after our present appearance is over. All the souls, including yours and mine, were created in the beginning when the universe was first created. There are no new souls. We are the same souls that built the pyramids, sailed the uncharted seas, walked the ancient roads, carved cities out of this planet's deserts, mountains and forests, and we have lived through the rise and fall of many nations and peoples. We are the ancient Egyptians, Carthaginians, Romans, Greeks, Hebrews and so on. Their wars were our wars. Their great cities and cultures were ours. Their virtues and victories, ours. Their sins and failures, ours. We are the men and women who have lived and died on this planet since humanity first appeared.

There is only one assembly of souls and we have been together since the very beginning—loving and fighting, sharing and stealing, caring and killing, forgiving and avenging, building and destroying. All of Earth's history is our history. In fact, all of the Universe's history is ours because our souls existed long before we ever came to earth.

One reason we have such difficulty with this idea is

our strong focus on the outer manifested world. For example, we think of ourselves as primarily BODIES and MINDS, which just may happen to have SPIRITS and SOULS. When, in fact, we are SPIRITS and SOULS which just happen to have physical bodies and conscious minds for only a relatively short time. Our outer, everyday selves are fresh, new and *temporary* expressions of a much more eternally enduring consciousness.

When we focus completely on our present life in our present meadow, our perspective is consequently narrowed to one life. If, however, our awareness is expanded to include the life, the consciousness, that has been in *all* the flowers—our soul's life, with all its experiences and memories—then our perspective is vast indeed and the horizons of our most recent birth and our coming death fall away to reveal a continuous life.

Spirit-Soul is that life, that consciousness, that was in each previous incarnation. Like the flower and its seed, our spirit-soul and its level of consciousness have appeared, disappeared and reappeared in many different meadows on earth. Within it are all the memories and influences of those experiences.

There is an ancient belief that the outer, physical world reflects the inner, spiritual world. Following this belief we should be able to look around the physical world and see a *reflection* of the spiritual world.

One such reflection can be found within our own bodies, for the idea of a continuous life is reflected in our bodies. We think of our bodies as "brand new," and in one sense, they are. But in another sense, they are extremely old. The cells that compose our present bodies have a direct, unbroken link with the cells of our hereditary ancestors. From the first bodies in our heredity line unto our present bodies there has been a continuous thread of life. Every cell in us today is linked directly with the cells of those past bodies from which ours are descendants. In this sense, our bodies are not brand new. They are actually the oldest bodies in a chain of countless others from which they have descended, and all the characteristics and experiences of those former bodies are having a significant effect on our present bodies. From human body to seed to human body again, life has been evolving toward our present bodies. We are walking around in a museum of our ancestors. Within our genetic structures are the records of ages of struggle and adaptation to life in this world.

However, physical analogies of spiritual realities can only go so far toward revealing the truth before they break down by the sheer limitations of the physical. Even though the basic characteristics of our bodies are fore-ordained through the ages of our ancestors' living and mating, our spirit-soul's entrance causes a uniqueness that expresses our soul. When the spirit of an individual soul enters into a physical body, it influences how that body forms and functions equally as much as the physical genes have influence. I find it amazing that many of us still believe that a single cell can reproduce the whole being of the offspring, its mind as well as its brain; its character, disposition, emotions, attitudes, innate talents and handicaps. Are chromosomes and cell division capable of creating not only the physical form but the mental, moral and emotional as well? Can they create the personality and spirit of the newborn?

We know that in the natural course of cell division specialization occurs, that the genetic code will dictate that some cells become kidneys, some the brain, etc. We also know that if we plant two seeds next to each other, one the seed of an oak tree and the other of an elm, that invariably they will grow to manifest their unique natures. The soil, water, heat and light is exactly the same for each seed. Even the power of growth is the same in each seed. Yet, as we all know, one will manifest the shape, leaf, flower and fruit of the oak, the other of the elm. Is all of this within the physical seed? It would appear so, and many of us argue that all of life is created and has its existence through physical forces only. However, in the *human* course of life and reproduction there occurs a phenomenon that does not follow this line of thinking, and it is within this exception that we have a glimpse of where the genetic influence ends and the non-physical spiritual influence begins.

In the case of identical twins, both sharing the same genetic code, we find we have two distinctly different individuals. They look exactly alike physically, but within them are different people. The physical does indeed follow its course, creating from within its own code a physical form reflecting that lineage, but then enters the spirit-soul from out of the other, non-physical dimensions of Whole-Life. This spirit-soul possesses all the uniqueness of an individual being, different from all others, even those within its own genetic family.

If we are to understand reincarnation, it is important to keep in mind that there are two distinct qualities to life: Essence and Form. Essence is the fundamental nature of life; form is the manifested expression of that nature. Form is what we see, essence is what we don't see. Essence is the invisible cause, form is the visible effect. An apple falling from a tree is the visible effect of a certain invisible cause or force called gravity. Although the force cannot be perceived by the physical senses, its effect is visible. No one has seen the Wind, only the effects it makes when it moves across our skin, or through the trees or over the seas. Electrical power can be brought into manifested life when we create the necessary conditions for it to flow, but no one knows from where it comes, nor has anyone ever seen electricity, only its manifested effects. All visible phenomena in this world are but the various expressions of the unseen essences of life.

We can see an example of this in water. The atoms of hydrogen and oxygen combined in a unique way appear in the outer form as water. Water can never be separated from hydrogen and oxygen, which are its essential parts. Its existence depends on its essential nature. We see it as water, but it is hydrogen and oxygen. In water we can gain a sense of the subtle relationship between the invisible and the visible, the essence and the form, the spirit-soul and the body. A waterdrop may manifest its essential nature in many forms: vapor, mist, cloud, then rain, snow and ice, again into steam; even in mud its presence can be manifested. However, it never dies, only changes its form—gaseous, liquid or solid—and it can take on these forms seemingly from out of nowhere. Its essential nature is always alive, whether visible or invisible.

All the characteristics of reality, a reality that includes essence as well as form, can be seen in the transitions of a waterdrop.

Our essence and its manifested form are like the waterdrop. We, our spiritual nature, can appear in the firm form of a physical body or the misty sweeps of a ghost. But whether visible or not, our essential self never dies. It simply changes how it expresses or manifests itself.

Now, I realize that all our Western minds are saying, "Hey, wait a minute. What about all the tangible evidence that we are strictly physical and have evolved from some rudimentary life-form that appeared in the waters of this planet millions of years ago? Are we to just ignore this huge body of evidence which clearly demonstrates evolution?"

EVOLUTION

The theory of Evolution is based on two principal factors: 1) The tendency of all living forms to vary and 2) the tendency of environment to influence that variation. Without the tendency to vary, evolution of any kind would be impossible. Evolving depends upon changing, varying. The second factor (i.e., environmental influence) depends on the law of "natural selection." In other words, the variation seeks to adapt toward favorable conditions. Therefore, a life-form will vary itself in order to suit the surrounding conditions or it will select environments that are favorable to itself. According to our evolution theory, the fundamental reason for this natural selection process is the "struggle for existence." Therefore, evolution depends on these four laws:

1) The tendency of living forms to vary.
2) The variation is influenced by the surrounding conditions.
3) Favorable conditions are constantly sought through natural selection.
4) The struggle for existence is the impulse that drives this process.

The problem with evolution is that, using these four laws, we try to explain *every* aspect of life: physical, mental, intellectual, moral and spiritual. From visible physical evidence we try to set up a model for all of life. But the theory of evolution will not explain all of life. Furthermore, the *first* cause of that innate tendency to vary which exists in every stage of all living forms is *not* the "struggle to exist." Despite enormous evidence to the contrary we continue to cling to the idea that variation and natural selection are caused by the struggle to exist. Let's explore this briefly.

Yes, in the lower forms of life the struggle for existence is a driving force. Even in our lower human nature we are driven by self-oriented motivations. The simple expression of animal nature which we observe in savages and lower animals does continue to appear in more complex ways as we gather into civilized groups of communities and nations. I think we'd all concede that the energy of the lower human nature is spent chiefly in the struggle for material existence. But there is another nature in all of us, a higher nature. Love of truth, mastery over passion, control of our senses, self-sacrifice, mercy, kindness, forgiveness, gentleness and giving one's life for another; all these are the expressions of a higher, moral, spiritual being. They certainly cannot be explained as developing from animal nature by means of a struggle for material existence. The moral, artistic, intellectual and spiritual nature of ourselves cannot be explained as an outgrowth or gradual development of the animal nature. Survival of the fittest and ruthless self-assertion which casts aside all competitors is simply not the primary motivation for man, as our evolution theories would lead us to believe.

The problem is that we no longer perceive that spiritual life *preceded* physical life. Nothing exists now that did not exist in the beginning. Like the waterdroplet, our essence has never *not* existed. Can that which now exists come out of non-existence? Can something come out of nothing? Our essential nature existed long before it ever manifested in this three-dimensional world that we are so totally wrapped-up with today. Life proceeded from out of the spirit into the mind and only then did it manifest itself in the physical.

The primary cause of the innate tendency to vary is the attempt of the life-essence *to become manifest*— for the potential to become actual, for the unseen to become seen. According to the principles upon which the theory of reincarnation is based, the essence of life *preceded* the forms of life. In other words, our spiritual nature preceded our physical nature. Along these lines of thought the theory of reincarnation builds its model of life.

INVOLUTION

One of the most fundamental concepts of reincarnation maintains that our spirit-souls *descended* from their original place through many levels of consciousness until we reached a point at which each of us made a conscious decision to "turn around" and begin the long ascent back again.

I used the term "original place" to identify our original location but it is really not a specific location per se. Rather, it is our original consciousness or level of awareness which was in close relationship with a Universal Consciousness. From this level of awareness and life we have *descended* to a level where we only have a very limited sense of the Universal and our relationship with the Cosmos, with Life. Furthermore, we have descended from a much higher "form" of being than we presently demonstrate. Our five senses of today are much reduced from what we have known in the past, and will expand to the 6th and higher senses as we continue the ascent.

This idea of an original descent from much higher levels of life is supported by the many myths and legends which tell of prehistoric civilizations that were actually *more* advanced than our present one. Most notable among these is the lost continent of Atlantis where it is said the inhibitants enjoyed air and space travel along with many more daily conveniences than we have today. Another example is Ancient Egypt which also presents us with technological power greater than that we possess today. Few modern engineers believe that pyramids can be constructed comparable to those in Giza. Even with our present high-technology we could not form or move those stones, or assemble them in a finished structure that would last four thousand years.

Now we are on the ascent. Once again we are becoming aware of the many dimensions to life. We are beginning to explore worlds beyond as well as within. Science and technology are rising faster than most of us can keep pace. Not surprisingly, religion and spiritual interest are also expanding.

We have descended into the lowest dimensions of life and consciousness from which we are now rising again to awaken to a much more fulfilling and meaningful level of consciousness and life. As we discussed earlier, essence descended until it was completely manifested in form, the potential became actual, the unseen, seen, and now it ascends again toward its first nature and true "place."

Let me simplify this whole line of thought by retelling the story of creation using the concepts of reincarnation.

THE BEGINNING

Imagine the universe before the beginning, before anything existed: nothing, absolutely nothing, emptiness for as far as you can see and hear in any direction you turn. Yet, the force that was going to begin the creation had to be there, somewhere. Somewhere within this pre-creation emptiness there had to exist the "first impulse," the "first cause."

One way for us to conceive of how there could be absolute emptiness before the beginning and yet something in this emptiness to cause the beginning is to imagine a consciousness similar to our own, except that this first consciousness would have been boundless, a Universal Consciousness. Before the beginning this Universal Consciousness would have been still, no thoughts or images in its Mind. It, and therefore the universe, was empty and still. But, like a consciousness without any thoughts, it was nevertheless alive and *possessed the potential* for thought, for creation. Using this example, when we looked through the pre-creation emptiness for the Creator, the "first impulse," we were actually standing within the Creator's infinite and quiet consciousness. The creation would begin much like a clear mind begins to conceive. Out of the invisible would come the visible because within the invisible lay the potential for the visible.

At some immeasurable moment this First Consciousness desired to express Itself, and stirring from Its silence, It began to conceive, to imagine and express Its inner promptings, and so the creation began.

During this wonderful awakening of the Universal Consciousness you and I and all the other souls were conceived. Within the Mind of what we have come to call God, we were first created. Unlike the other creations, we were given independent will and individual consciousness to use as we desired. This was done in the hope that we would become the companions of the First Consciousness.

Consciousness and free will were the greatest qualities given any creation but they came with equally great responsibility for their use or neglect. Of course, the all-knowing Universal One knew the potential dangers in giving beings complete freedom to do as they desired. However, the potential joy of sharing life with *true* companions, not servants, was deemed worth the risk. Therefore, each of these new free-willed beings (our spirit-souls) would simply have to learn to take charge of themselves and to subdue any harmful desires in order to live in harmony with the other companions and the Creator. To do otherwise would only bring suffering and loneliness.

It's important for us to realize that at this point in our existence we did *not* have physical bodies like we do today. All of what I've just described occurred within the Mind of God. Consequently, its "form" resembled that of thoughts rather than physical objects. In the very beginning we were individual points of consciousness within the one great Universal Consciousness.

At first, we were still, our wills content to observe the wonders of the creation as they flowed from the Mind of God. In these early periods we were so much a part of the Creator's Consciousness that we were one with It, virtually indistinguishable from It. However, it wasn't long before some of us began to use our wills and express ourselves, taking part in the creation. At first, we simply imitated the Creator, but eventually we gained experience and with experience came knowledge and confidence. Then, we truly began to create, adding new dimensions to the creation, much like a second voice adds to a song by singing in harmony with the main melody.

This was a wonderful, deeply fulfilling time. It was exactly why we had been created—to share in and contribute to the great expression of Life and to be Its companions. To fulfill this purpose we were created in the image of the Creator: consciousness with freedom to think, to act and to choose; capable of conceiving, perceiving and remembering, and most of all, capable of communicating directly with the Creator and the other companions.

However, as we continued to use our godly powers we became more fascinated with them. We began to focus more and more on our own creations and we became less concerned with and attentive to their harmony with the Creator, with the Whole. The more we thought of just ourselves and our own desires with less and less regard for the Whole, the more self-centered we became, until we eventually perceived ourselves as separate from the Whole.

Of course, this sense of separation was all in our heads, so to speak, because there really was no way one could exist outside of the Whole. It was more a result of our sustained focus of attention on ourselves and our self-interest that resulted in this heightened sense of a distinct and separate self.

This was the beginning of trouble. It led to a very long fall for us. A fall that eventually left us feeling alone and separate from the rest of life, even to the point that we, who were actually companions and co-creators with the Universal Creator, came to think of ourselves as little more than dust-like creatures, descendents of apes and inhabitants of an insignificant planet in this endless and diverse universe.

To know ourselves to be ourselves and yet one with the Whole was the ideal condition, but the centering of awareness on self alone resulted in a sense of separation from the Whole. The more we exercised our individual consciousness and free-will for self-interest, self-gratification, self-glorification and self-consciousness, the more we heightened our sense of self, a self apart from the Whole.

The resulting loss of contact with the source of our

life and the purpose for our existence was the beginning of evil. Without a clear sense of our relationship to the rest of life and our purpose for being, many of us began to use free-will in ways that were never meant to be and others simply let themselves be carried along with the current of life, abdicating their gift of free-will to the will of others. In both cases, our naive curiosity, combined with an almost reckless disregard for the consequences of our actions and thoughts, and our relentless self-seeking desires caused us to do and experience many things that we would come to regret, things that would change us forever.

In the early stages of our descent from original consciousness we gradually lost the expanse of awareness that was ours to enjoy. Instead, we focused our attention more on the images that flowed out of the Mind of God and our own creative minds, becoming enchanted with them. Some of us willingly sought the enchantment, others let themselves be pulled into it.

This change occurred much like a person walks into a room with a television on and before long is so caught-up in the images, sounds and stories on the TV that he or she becomes oblivious to what is going on in the room. Trying to communicate with the person watching TV or involve them in the activities of others in the house becomes difficult. Their complete consciousness and will is now subordinated to the events of the television world. In a similar way, our souls become caught-up in the stream of creation, losing awareness of our true nature and purpose. To keep the stimulus interesting, and thereby maintain the sensation, we moved through the various dimensions of creation, much like a person would turn from channel to channel, watching a program on one channel, then moving to a program on another—each providing some new opportunity to continue the stimulation and enchantment.

Maintaining our attunement and companionship with the Creator wasn't so important any longer. We simply lived our lives through the endless stories and activities of the worlds before us. Only rarely would our soul come back into the room of its original consciousness and again become aware of the life that exists beyond the television world, the manifested world. Even when our soul's focus returned to the room, the effects of television stayed with us. In a real sense, we had become possessed by activity. In the beginning we couldn't get enough of it. Only later, when the scenes and sensations began to repeat themselves, did we begin to seek something more substantial, more eternally fulfilling and satisfying. By then, we had become very different beings. Our divine nature had descended into matter and become human. Now, we possessed two opposing natures, one divine and the other human, one composed of spirit and the other of flesh.

To paraphrase the late Edgar Cayce—Man no longer walked after the ways of the spirit but after the ways of the flesh, and so he began a long journey that led to the death of his spiritual awareness. Our spiritual being died in the sense that we no longer perceived it as a part of us. Therefore, for all intents and purposes, it was dead. We had become completely physical. Our spirit-soul had pushed its way completely into manifestation only to lose track of where it had come from and what it truly was.

These early experiences would prove to become tremendous obstacles to the fulfillment of our original purpose for being. Nevertheless, with every mistake, every wrong turn, every misuse of free-will the Creator prepared opportunities for the souls to change their ways, change their minds, and choose again the original course, the original consciousness. No soul was to be lost forever, for it was never intended by the Creator that any should be lost. It simply did not create companions only to lose them to the darkenss of a narrower, lower consciousness. Therefore, with every action and thought that confuses or harms a soul It provides a remedy, a way out, a solution—but the soul must CHOOSE to accept the opportunity. No one, not the Creator or any other companion, can override the free-will of a soul. This is the birthright of each soul, and what one does with it is theirs to do. To interfere with a soul's free-will is to take away its opportunity to become what it was created to be. A companion, a true companion, is one who *chooses* to be with you, not one who *has* to be with you, and this is the birthright of each soul. Each has an opportunity to freely choose to companion with the Universal Consciousness, the Ineffable One who gave us life. Unfortunately, this same freedom also provides the soul with an opportunity to rebel against this very One and to do much harm to itself and others.

THE UNIVERSAL LAW

To insure that things didn't get too far out of hand, the Creator established a universal law to which all of life would be subject. This law of the universe is simple: As we sow, so shall we reap. What we do with our consciousness and free-will, both to ourselves and others, we must meet; perhaps not today or tomorrow, but without any exceptions, we will experience the effects of our actions.

The thoughts and actions of each individual consciousness affect the others and the Whole, and in order to insure that chaos does not become the ultimate state of things, the law works its way to reveal to each soul the effects of their actions and thoughts.

There is no escaping this law. No matter how great one is or how lowly, all are subject to it. And, contrary to what most of us have come to believe, not the slightest thought or littlest act is commited in secret. Nothing is conceived in an individual mind that does not make an impression on the Universal Mind. There are no secrets, nothing is hidden, nothing is forgotten. That does not mean that it can't be suppressed in the subconscious for long periods of time, but eventually and inevitably it will surface and must be dealt with.

However, the universal law is not as ominous as it may sound for it is actually the great teacher of man. The real purpose for the law is not retribution and punishment, but education. Ultimately, through the natural working of the law, each soul comes again to the crossroads of its past desires, actions, thoughts and words. In this way it has an opportunity to consider again the effects of its previous use or neglect of free-will and to decide again how it will use this power, this incredible gift. The law is simply an impersonal process by which each soul has an opportunity to change its ways, its mind, through experiencing the effects of its previous decisions and omissions. The intention of the law is to provide each soul with an insight into just how its desires, actions, thoughts and words affect itself, others and the Whole.

All of life is bound by the law of cause and effect, action and reaction. As we align our individual wills with this law we begin to grasp hold of the power to regain that which we have lost. By making present choices that reflect our higher natures rather than our lower natures, we begin to effect a change within ourselves and our destiny. From out of the ashes of death our reawakened spiritual consciousness rises again to its life and purpose.

The goal is to know ourselves to be our true selves, and yet one with the Whole in harmony and companionship.

PAST LIFE MEMORY

If all of this is true, why don't we remember any of this amazing scenerio that was just described? Could we possibly have experienced all of this and not remember any of it? Actually, *we* have not experienced it. Our outer, everyday selves have not been alive before. Our bodies, conscious minds and personalities are new expressions from out of our souls. Consequently, the past lives are not ours per se, they are our soul's. In order to get a better idea of just how this can be, let's look at the twin transitions of birth and death.

Upon the death of the body, the mind and soul of the individual are released from physical form. Depending on its level of consciousness, the individual will either perceive this transition or, in its ignorance, become bewildered and confused. However, it will no longer be able to communicate with its friends and relatives that remain incarnate. It can neither vibrate the vocal cords of the now dead body to produce sounds that vibrate the physical ear drums of the incarnate, nor can it reflect light off the surface of its former body so that it can be seen by carnal eyes. Usually this initial inability to communicate causes the individual to realize that "death" has occurred. When this realization reaches its ultimate enlightenment, the conscious mind begins to relinguish its hold on consciousness, much in the same way it did in sleep. Subsequently, the subconscious mind rises to become the more prominant consciousness in the next dimension of life, as it did during sleep. Eventually, the subconscious mind, which is primarily a fourth-dimensional mind, will become the operative mind for life beyond death.

The strongest thought, aspiration or desire which arose during the most recent incarnate life will become dominant at the time of death, much in the same way that the strongest thoughts and desires of the day often affect the dreams during the night. These aspirations will act like a force upon the soul. As the soul takes stock of the life, it will be moved by the force of these aspirations, and seek or be driven toward its next environment by this force; ever reaching for or being forced to accept that environment which helps it achieve its purpose for existence.

How all of this occurs depends a great deal on the level of spiritual awareness possessed by the dying

PATH OF REINCARNATION

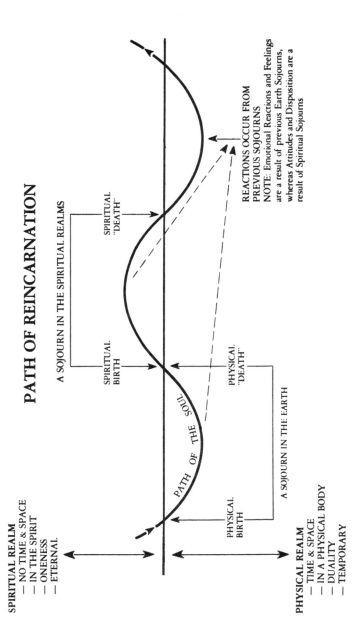

SPIRITUAL REALM
— NO TIME & SPACE
— IN THE SPIRIT
— ONENESS
— ETERNAL

A SOJOURN IN THE SPIRITUAL REALMS

SPIRITUAL "DEATH"

SPIRITUAL BIRTH

PATH OF THE SOUL

PHYSICAL "DEATH"

A SOJOURN IN THE EARTH

PHYSICAL BIRTH

PHYSICAL REALM
— TIME & SPACE
— IN A PHYSICAL BODY
— DUALITY
— TEMPORARY

REACTIONS OCCUR FROM PREVIOUS SOJOURNS
NOTE: Emotional Reactions and Feelings are a result of previous Earth Sojourns, whereas Attitudes and Disposition are a result of Spiritual Sojourns

individual. In cases where there is little or no aware-ness, the forces of direction are involuntary, ruled by the law of cause and effect. However, where there is some awareness of the spiritual, the soul can again use its divine gift of free-will in this process of transi-tion and movement toward another dimension of life.

In whatever environ it seeks or finds itself, the spirit-soul may sojourn for only a few earth-years or for many thousands before it returns to earth.

Here's where the memory is affected. In order to reincarnate and function again in the earth's dimen-sion, the soul must develop another three-dimensional consciousness to enter a new three-dimensional body. Since the new conscious mind is neither the previous consciousness of the realms beyond physi-cal life nor the previous earth-life conscious mind of the former incarnation, it does not possess of itself any memories of previous lives. The memories are in the subconscious, the soul's mind, and it is here that we must seek to know how reincarnation is affecting us in our present life.

Now, we might well ask, "How then can the experi-ences of our soul affect us when we have no memory of these experiences?" It happens much in the same way that a father's experiences affect his son. Even though the son does not possess the memories of his father's experiences, he will be hard pressed to avoid the influences of these experiences on his own life. If the son wishes to know how his father's experiences are affecting him, then he must seek-out the father and discover what life has been like for him. What were the experiences in the father's life that shaped his attitudes, emotions, opinions, beliefs and person-ality. In a similar way, our soul's experiences are not our memories, but since we are the offspring of our soul we can't help but be influenced by them. If we are to understand our innate urges and dispositions we must seek-out our soul and learn of its experiences. Only then can we completely understand why we are the way we are, and why our life is the way it is.

CHAPTER TWO
REINCARNATION &
OUR PRESENT RELATIONSHIPS

We are like rivers. On the surface we are all shiny and clear, shimmering with freshness and life, but deep within us run unseen currents of powerful influence. These deep currents are the cumulative effects of ages of soul-life and many incarnations into this world. These unseen currents cause us to love one person and despise another. They cause us to feel wonderful vibrations with a particular individual in one aspect of our life only to feel awkward and uncomfortable with that same person in another aspect of our life. Patterns and habits have formed deep within our inner-consciousness and shape the way we interact with people around us. On the surface all is new and bright, but deep below lie powerful unseen currents of soul-memories and desires.

Everyone involved in our *present* life was very likely involved in our *past* lives. Actually, it is likely they have been involved in *many* of our past lives. Our parents, brothers and sisters, spouses, children, friends, colleagues, bosses and employees, and on and on, even our enemies have been sharing life with us long before this present lifetime.

The effects of these many past-life experiences are reflected in the circumstances that now surround our present relationships. Our soul's memories of past-life activities with these other souls shape our innate reactions to them. Of course, *their* memories of our past-life actions influence how they react to us. Through the same eyes that our personality looks at this life, our soul looks at life, but our soul looks with a memory covering centuries of passion and adventure, caring and love, hatred and revenge, doubt and fear. When we feel a seemingly unfounded fondness for another person, it is very likely due to our soul's memory of the positive role they played in our past lives. When we react with what seems to be unfounded revulsion or hatred toward another person, you can be pretty sure it is because of our soul's memory of their past actions against us or our loved ones.

However, in life the influences of past-life actions are rarely so clear cut. Often those with whom we have had many good lives and relationships are the same people with whom we have had many problems and disagreements. Therefore, in our present life we will find that our "good karma" with each other is often mixed with some "bad karma." It's rare that a past-life relationship had every aspect of life in good, clear focus. Those aspects that we did develop well in our past lives will give us much pleasure and support in our present life. Those aspects which we did not have in proper focus will give us opportunities for some pain and growth in our present relationship together. Avoiding these influences is simply not possible. Whether we like it or not, the Universal Law constantly brings before each of us the meeting of our past use of free will and consciousness. What we have done to other souls and they have done to us is reflected in the circumstances surrounding our present relationships and the basic, innate urges, attitudes and emotions we feel toward them.

SOUL GROUPS

These basic ideas of past relationships and their present influences are not only true of our individual relationships but also of our group relationships. From the beginning our souls have tended to travel together in groups, and the very act of traveling together for such long periods creates forces of attraction that help to maintain and build on these group relationships. Nearly all the souls on the planet today were together in past ages of human history. As a result, the relationships among the peoples of the world today are a reflection of their past activities with each other. The souls who came into this planetary system and entered the realms of consciousness associated with this region of the cosmos comprise our largest soul group. This group can then be divided into the subgroups we call "the generations," containing souls who move through the natural cycles of this life together. Within the generations we divide into the various nations, cultures, races, religions, etc., that have formed during ages of interaction together. These groups then divide into the groups of souls who share similar philosophies, ideas, purposes, aspirations and attitudes *within* the nations, cultures, races, religions, etc. From here the soul groups further divide into the many smaller groups of personal relationships: communities, families, businesses, teams, schools and so on.

Soul groups create an affinity among their members by not only the cumulative experiences they share, but also through their collective memory of how life has been for them and what they have come to mutually desire out of life. In a manner of speaking, the groups form a distinct collective consciousness and spirit, much like the souls who gave us "the spirit of '76." That spirit, that collective expression that we now identify as "the spirit of '76" reflected that soul-group's collective consciousness, comprised of their mutual memories, hopes, attitudes and purposes.

Soul groups are not rigid or static. Any individual soul can use its free will to seek an experience in another group. There are many cases where souls changed political allegiance, race, or religion from one lifetime to another. Neither do the generations incarnate in strict, rigid patterns. A member of one generation may come again with another generation. For example, two members of a family group who were father and son in one life may change positions and become son and father in another, or grandfather and grandson. They may even choose to be in the same generation in an incarnation, as brothers, for example. However, they may even choose *not* to be in the same family again.

Although the soul groups are fairly well established and have significant pull on the individuals within them, they are not rigid nor do they have greater influence than a soul's will to change.

Generally though, soul groups cycle in and out of this world together and, therefore, at approximately the same time. (I am speaking in eras and ages, not days or years.) This is particularly evident in the past-life "readings" of Edgar Cayce (see Appendix for details on Edgar Cayce). After giving thousands of past-life experiences for individuals, some recurring sequences of incarnations became evident. Many of his past-life "readings," as they were called, were for souls who fell into one of two major soul groups and naturally followed their cycles of incarnating. Notice in the following listing that the two groups were sometimes in the Earth at the same periods, but in different nations and geographic locations. Not surprisingly, Edgar Cayce and those who worked closely with him also traveled with one of these two groups.

THE INCARNATIONS OF TWO MAJOR SOUL
GROUPS FOUND IN THE EDGAR CAYCE READINGS
Group 1:
Early Atlantis
Early Ancient Egypt
Persia (during the time of Croseus I, II)
Palestine
The Crusades
Colonial America
Group 2:
Late Atlantis
Late Ancient Egypt
Early Greece
Rome (during the time of Christ)
France (during the time of Louis XIV, XV, XVI)
The American Civil War

Of course, these are only the most significant incarnations for these souls; they would most probably have incarnated many more times than the list indicates. There were other incarnation-sequences given, but the majority of his readings were for souls who typically cycled with one of these two major groups. There were also some significant exceptions to this pattern that we should take a look at. Some souls did not always incarnate when their group did, choosing instead to skip a cycle or enter with another group, though they usually rejoined their original group eventually. Others, though cycling into the Earth-plane with their group, did not actually incarnate, i.e., did not enter into a body; rather they stayed in the spirit and helped from a higher vantage-point while the others incarnated. One example of this comes from an Edgar Cayce reading for a woman who wanted to know why she hadn't been given an incarnation during the Palestine era in which her present son and husband had incarnated. She was told that she was there, but not in the flesh. She was, as some of us would term it today, a "guardian angel" for her present son while he lived and worked in that period.

A group of souls may find themselves together again and yet not one of them desired it to be so. In these cases, it is often the forces of the Universal Law that cause them to come together. For better or for worse they now have to meet the effects of their past actions with each other. Hopefully, this confrontation leads to a resolution of their karma or at least a recognition of how their past actions with each other have caused the present predicament and a resolve not to act that way again.

Both in individual and group relationships, the karmic effects of past actions with others can create some very difficult, even terrible situations. The meeting can result in murder, rape, torture and other atrocities. Even in lesser cases karmic effect can result in back-biting, back-stabbing, bickering, fighting and other turmoils. Imagine what might happen if the universal forces of cause and effect brought together the souls of the Roman Coliseum and the souls they fed to the lions, or the Conquistadors and the Incas and Aztecs, or the Nazis and Jews.

The same cause-and-effect forces play a part in individual lives, too. Imagine if the law brought together a soul who killed another in a family quarrel with the victim of that quarrel. What about a soul who betrayed another's trust or love? What would be the reaction toward one another in this present life? When lives are heavily burdened by the negative effects of their past actions, their present experience is often tragic, occasionally their lives may appear to be wasted senselessly. However, from the soul's perspective a single incarnation is a learning-experience and an opportunity to resolve past actions that are now holding the soul back from its fuller life. One physical life is not the ultimate living experience for the soul. It is an opportunity to resolve the burdens past actions have placed upon our souls and to clear away the many ideas that continue to confuse and limit us. So even though the seventy or eighty years that comprise the average lifetime seem so very singular and final, it is only a temporary sojourn, a brief experience along an infinite path of soul-life.

Of course, all the good that has been experienced between the various souls and soul groups has just as strong an effect on the present situations and opportunities as evil, and when we focus on this "good karma" we often find better ways to resolve the negative influences.

SOUL MATES

A "soul mate" is really nothing more than a soul, or souls (and there may be several of them) with whom we have *closely* shared so many lifetimes that we now resonate to the same pitch, so to speak. We understand each other like no one else could hope to, simply because of the ages of sharing life together. This acquired understanding gives soul mates the capacity to help each other in ways that would be difficult without the deep bonding that has occurred through the ages.

Soul mates often help each other reach their highest potential, and though this is not automatic and each will still have to apply themselves to making the present relationship the best it can be, their deep inner-knowing of each other gives them a distinct advantage. However, being soul mates doesn't automatically mean that they see eye-to-eye on everything. In fact, they are usually more like complements one-to-another than duplicates of each other, each one bringing to the relationship something the other is missing, thereby rounding-out the realtionship and giving each of them more than they have separately.

When soul mates are together, they form a dynamic bond and provide a source of strength for one another that is very hard to find in this world. It is important to realize, however, that since they are *souls* who have had many incarnations together and *not personalities* that have lived together before this life, they can presently be in either physical sex and interact with each other in any number of different types of relationships. There is a strong tendency to think of soul mates only in the sense of lovers and marriage mates, but they can also be business partners, parents, siblings, teammates, friends, etc. If, however, they happened to have been lovers and mates in many, many past lives, it will be very hard for them to avoid at least a romantic interlude in the present life. There would simply be too much magnetism for them to easily ignore each other and the physical attraction. If, on the other hand, they have been close friends or family members throughout their incarnations, then the present attraction would be toward this same type of relationship. The point is, a soul-mate is not always a sexual mate.

Another important point about soul mates is that the *true* mate of every soul is its Original Companion, its Creator, who gave each soul life for the very purpose of being eternal companions with the Creator, the Universal Consciousness, God. As far as the sexual dynamics of soul mating, it's important to keep in mind that in the heavenly home we (our souls) "neither marry nor are given in marriage." As souls, we are actually siblings in the Universal Family. Therefore, even though soul mates may give each other the support that is needed and deserved in this difficult world, which may include healthy, intimate, sexual companionship, they are ultimately brother and sisters in the spiritual realms.

TWIN SOULS

This brings us to one of the strangest concepts concerning soul relationships, that of "Twin Souls." Prior to entering the duality of the earth a soul is androgenous, possessing both the male and female sexual forces within one complete soul. As the soul enters the world it selects one of the two sexual natures and *projects* the unique characteristics of this sex while incarnate. Usually, the sex projected by the soul is the same as the physical body into which it incarnates, but not always. Sometimes a soul can be manifesting its female nature and yet incarnate in a male body, resulting in an effeminate male, and the reverse can occur, as well. How all of this leads us to the twin-soul concept is that, as difficult as it may be to understand, the unmanifested sexual part of our soul can actually incarnate while we are incarnate. In other words, our soul, which is much more complex than we have imagined, is capable of separating its dual sexual nature into two separate and distinct entities, one male and the other female, and each of these two entities can incarnate into the Earth at the same time in separate bodies that usually correspond to their sex. Consequently, somewhere out there in the physical world is literally our other half! The *other sexual part of our soul* may actually be physically living in the world today.

There are some examples of this in the Cayce readings. One of the more notable is a group of four souls who, in their present incarnation, were husband, wife, eldest son and a female business associate who was also a very close friend of the family. The husband was told through his readings that his present wife was his *soul-mate* and that his life would never have reached its fullest potential without her. However, it went on to say that the female business associate and close friend of the family was his *twin soul;* in other words, she was the other sexual half of his complete soul. Furthermore, his wife's twin soul was their eldest son! I realize how bizarre all of this sounds, but the dynamics and dimensions of life are simply far greater than we have yet imagined. Of course, not all examples are as closely knit as this example from the Cayce readings. Generally, the twin soul relationship is presently found among spouses, friends, occasionally as parent and child, and sometimes the twin soul isn't even incarnate at the same time. However, there does seem to be a pattern that most twin-soul relationships follow: In their early incarnations together they tend to be mates or at least seek a lover's relationship with each other, while in their later incarnations with each other they tend to seek less sexually involved relationships and more workrelated activities together, especially when the work has a soul purpose. This could be due to the involution/evolution process where, in the early periods of the descent into materiality they tended to continue their self-seeking, self-satisfying pursuits, but on the ascent toward a return to spirituality they tend to seek more holistic purposes and relationships. That is not to say that all present sexual relationships are self-seeking. From the Cayce material we find healthy support for marriage and home, and all the natural sexual aspects that are a part of the union of two in love and mutual caring.

Let's look at how these ideas of soul groups, soul

mates and twin souls actually fit into the esoteric view of life.

PARENTS & CHILDREN

First of all, as hard as it may be for us to believe, each soul actually chooses its parents—with one exception. If a soul has so abused its gift of free will then it comes under the strong influence of the universal law and is carried along on the force of its past actions into present relationships that it simply must face up to. Of course, no soul is given more than it can handle, not that it won't suffer, but it won't be totally lost or destroyed by the burdens of its karma. Generally though, *we choose our parents prior to entering this life.*

As we would expect, souls who have had experiences together in past lives will have a stronger attraction for each other than souls who have had no past experiences together. Even if souls aren't particularly fond of each other they still tend to be drawn together by the forces of their knowing one another. Furthermore, if we have a specific purpose for incarnating, and most of us do, then we will be seeking others who are a part of fulfilling our purpose or who can at least contribute to it. Again, this doesn't mean that the early family life will be all hugs and kisses. In every relationship one can find advantages and disadvantages, and in order to enjoy the advantages one must accept the disadvantages. In fact, in many cases, the disadvantages lead to or create the opportunities for the advantages. When a soul is trying to decide which channels (parents) would be best for it to enter this world through, it has to accept the limitations of this particular family as well as the opportunities.

From the spiritual realm Earth-life appears much like a river when viewed from high above, a "bird's eye view." The soul who is deciding which channels to enter through sees the river in all its vastness, with many tributaries and branches, and it sees where the parents' boat is on this river of life. In this way it has an overview of what life will be like with these parents. However, because the river of life has many side-routes, the incoming soul can only see the strongest current in the parents' lives. It can't be sure that one of the free-willed parents won't change its mind and begin pursuing a different course, or that the currents won't change course and thereby change the family's future. It can't even be certain that it won't change its own mind once it gets into the boat.

Destiny and fate do exist, and they exist side-by-side with free will. The effects of our past actions have an inertia that carries over into our present life and shapes it, thereby creating our destiny. However, nothing surpasses the power of our soul's divinely-given free will. At any time we can use our will to change directions, change attitudes, change purposes, change anything! In this way, our lives are both fatal-istically foreshadowed by the cause-and-effect forces of our past use of free will, and yet amenable to change by our present use of free will.

Therefore, the incoming soul can only see the general course of the family's riverboat, it can't be sure the family will stay the course.

The incarnate parents also have significant influ-ence as to which soul enters through them. Their daily thoughts, desires and purposes create a beacon for souls who respond to these energies. This is particularly true of the mother. Her daily activities and inner-thoughts during the gestation period create a field much like a magnet would, and souls who respond to that field come near her to see if they can accept the opportunity she offers. As you would expect, more than one soul may be attracted to the mother-to-be. In these cases, the forces of cause-and-effect, the will-power and desire of the mother and the souls wanting to incarnate combine to make the selection. The other souls who wanted to come in through this same channel may well come in during a later pregnancy, becoming siblings of the souls who entered first, or they may go on to other families with whom friendships or other blood relationships would naturally form.

The soul generally enters the baby body at or near the time of birth. In one unusual case in the Cayce readings, the soul did not enter for two days after the birth of the baby body! When asked why it didn't enter for such a long time, Cayce responded that the soul knew it was going to be a very difficult life and it wasn't sure it wanted to go through with it. Cayce was then asked what kept the baby body alive for two days while the soul wrestled with its decision and he responded, "the spirit." For Cayce, the soul was the entity, with all its personal memories and aspirations, and the spirit was the life force.

According to the metaphysical work of Rudolf Steiner, the soul actually incarnates in four stages: 1) A first level of consciousness enters at or near the time of birth. 2) A second and greater level of consciousness enters around the time the child cuts its first teeth. 3) A third level enters during puberty. And, 4) The final and complete entry of the soul occurs around the age of twenty-one.

Most sources agree that the first few years of life are primarily devoted to developing the physical body. Then the years from two to seven shape much of the child's sense of self and its view of the world. Around the time of puberty the karmic influences begin to take hold on the incarnation and influence the child and his or her relationships. Around the age of 21 the individual begins to assume its major course through life. From here on the life progresses through a series of experiences and decision crossroads. These occur in natural and identifiable cycles, the most influential being the Seven Year Cycle: 1-7, 8-14, 15-21, 21-28, and so on. Notice how these cycles coincide with the general metaphysical cycles of: birth, seven years of age, puberty (though puberty usually occurs before 14, it is fulfilled at or near this age), and twenty-one years of age.

Furthermore, each soul experiences life in two primary arenas: 1) The inner world of self, which includes one's mental and emotional being and its physical body. 2) The outer arena of life's unique circumstances, including the social, economic, racial, national and religious situation, all of which are generally set at birth and the outer world has pre-structured in specific ways.

In order for us to really understand how all of this occurs in life and relates to our own lives, we need to look at some real-life examples. The next two chapters tell the stories of past lives and present relationships for a number of individuals.

CHAPTER THREE
EXAMPLES OF PAST LIVES
AND PRESENT RELATIONSHIPS

Let's look at some family examples from the Cayce material. Like most young girls, Linda Mills wanted to fall in love with a wonderful man, have a family and live a rich, full life. When she met her future husband, she was genuinely attracted to him, yet she knew he wasn't everything she had dreamed about. She especially didn't like his tendency to make decisions for her. Nevertheless, their love for each other was strong and they felt a deep mutual attraction. They were also quite comfortable with each other around their friends and family. They married and had two daughters. For Linda, the first daughter was a joy. Throughout the pregnancy and after the birth she and her new baby were very comfortable and happy with each other. They spent many wonderful moments together nursing and rocking while Linda softly hummed lullabies. However, her second daughter was quite a different story. The pregnancy was uncomfortable, filled with sickness and stress, and after the birth she and the little girl just never seemed to get into sync with each other. The

child couldn't breast-feed like her first, actually becoming sick from the breast milk, and formula was
substituted. She also didn't enjoy being held or rocked
like the first child. However, the second daughter was
very comfortable with her daddy, and as she grew up
this became even more evident. She was "daddy's little
girl" while the first child was certainly mommy's. When
this couple and their family received a "past-life reading" from Edgar Cayce the cause of many of their
present experiences with each other became quite
clear.

Linda and her husband had been husband and wife
before, but in the incarnation just prior to this one,
they were father and daughter. His tendency to make
decisions for her and control her life was a carry-over
from being the father. In that past life Linda had been
a rather wild and rebellious child. This was due in part
to her resentment for the man who had always been
her equal now being her father. It was a difficult life for
him, too. Raising her was very hard, especially after the
death of his wife in that lifetime. All these feelings
carried-over into their present life and marriage. As for
the children, the *first* daughter had been Linda's close
friend through many lifetimes and this love and friendship continued in the present life. In the most recent
past-life, the first daughter had helped Linda deal with
the problems she, Linda, was having with her father,
and now as the daughter she would do so again in this
lifetime with Linda's husband. However, the *second*
daughter had been Linda's husband's lover in many
past lives and this created an enmity between them in
the present, even to the point that Linda's milk made
her sick. Neither did she want Linda's love and comfort

as much as she did her present father's! Now the father and his second daughter would have to learn to love each other in a much different way or break one of the strictest taboos, incest.

As we can see, the deep currents of their souls' past experiences were playing a significant role in their present relationships. According to the Cayce readings, their goal now, from their souls' point of view, was to live together again and make an effort to accentuate the love and virtues and minimize the resentments and bad habits they carried with them as a result of their past.

In another case, despite all his efforts to ignore or resist it, Michael Parks was afraid of the dark. His fear of the dark was not like most children, he was deathly afraid, to the point of suffocating if left in the dark too long. As far as he and his parents could recall, his childhood was rather normal and nothing had occurred that might have caused this fear. Yet, for all of his childhood life in his parents' home, everyone had to be aware of his fear and take precautions to insure that he was never inadvertently left alone in a dark room or house. His parents were very tolerant of his fear. They cared for him in every way and were unusually understanding and sympathetic. Later, when he married and started a home and family of his own, his wife had to assume the burden of his fear. She too proved to be very patient with him. Together they worked out an elaborate scheme whereby he could go to bed with the lights on and she would come to bed after he had fallen asleep. Only then would she turn the lights off so she could fall asleep. Even so, if he awoke during the night, he would become extremely anxious and uncomfortable. He would have to fight to keep himself from panicking in order to turn on his bedside light. But once this had occurred the only way he could get back to sleep was to go into the living room, turn on all the lights and sleep on the couch, knowing the lights would be on while he slept.

One night Michael awoke from a terrifying dream. This dream was to be the beginning of his conquering the fear. He dreamt he was in a dark dungeon surrounded by wet stone walls that went up so high he could not see where they ended. There was absolutely no way out and no one was coming to help him. As he stood there he began to cry. He cried so long and hard that the cell began to fill with his tears. When he noticed the tear-water was up to his chest, he tried to stop crying but he couldn't get hold of himself, it all seemed too horribly fixed, so unchangable that he felt completely trapped without hope of ever seeing light or life again. Eventually, the pool of tears reached his nose and he had to stand on his tip-toes to breathe, yet he continued to cry. Slowly he allowed himself to ease under the water, drifting into a sorrowful, lonely dream of letting go, surrendering his will to the reality of his predicament. At this point he awoke from the dream. The sheets were soaked and his body was covered with chilly sweat. When he told his wife and his parents the dream they cried and were very upset by it. However, Michael was beginning to feel pretty good about the dream. In fact, he noticed his fear of the dark had actually diminished since the dream. It was as though something in the dream had healed and changed him.

About a year later he happened to take part in a series of exercises for recalling past-life experiences.

From the information he received during these exercises and several more dreams over the next two years, he began to understand why he was afraid of the dark.

In a previous incarnation he had been a renegade from the courts and causes of Louis XIV. So violent and disruptive were his counter-attacks against the king that he became the most wanted man in France. His raids destroyed many of the king's storehouses, and his ability to elude capture created a great deal of hatred among the king's soldiers charged with capturing him. One day they did capture him and in retaliation for his actions and also as a result of the solders' frustration over trying to stop him, they threw him into the bottom of a well-like dungeon, covered it and left him there to die a slow death. In this terrible place, in complete darkness he managed to survive for weeks. In the beginning he was sure his friends and wife would come to his rescue. But as time went by he realized that no one was coming and he lost hope and died. In the latter days of this ordeal he lost all sense of time and his mind began to fall apart. He could no longer be sure of what was real and what was illusion. But the worst part of his ordeal was the unrelenting darkness and confinement. This was what his soul remembered the most, and feared.

Just as we would expect, his current parents and wife, who helped him deal with this fear in this present life, were the very people he had counted on to rescue him from the dungeon. His father and his wife were his close friends and colleagues-in-arms, while his present mother had been his wife in the French incarnation. They didn't go to his rescue because he had become so notorious that it would have been too risky to attempt to save him without being captured and thrown into the dungeon with him. To a great degree, his own actions had brought him to this end, and yet, his parents and wife regretted that they at least didn't try to rescue him. His dream in this life was too much for his parents and wife to hear without deeply reacting to his ordeal. However, once his own soul had relieved itself of this horrible memory by remembering in the dream, it seemed to release him from the fear.

In another, less dramatic case, a man who had fallen in love with a divorcee who had a child from a previous marriage, found himself struggling with his feelings. He eventually married the woman and tried to be the best step-father to her child that he could, but when he discovered that he could not have children himself, he felt cheated and had to fight feelings of resentment toward his wife and her child. When he received a past-life reading from Edgar Cayce, he was told that in a previous incarnation in ancient Greece he had been married to the same woman. In that life she was the one who couldn't have children and though he knew how sensitive she was to this limitation of hers and its implications in those days, he chose to have a second wife and have a child by her. He then brought this second wife and child to live in the same house as his barren first wife. She had to live with the shame and humiliation of this situation while they enjoyed the happiness of their little family. Now, he was meeting himself in this life. Now, he couldn't have children and had to live in a house with his wife's child and their natural happiness together.

Of course, if she now chose to take advantage of the present situation and make life as miserable as possible for him, she could be setting herself up for future destiny of some sadness. The law is very impersonal. What one does, one experiences, without exception. If she chose to help her husband meet his fate as best she could, she would heal many wounds and free herself at the same time.

In another case, a beautiful woman from the modern cosmopolitan life of a big city came to Cayce and described her tragic predicament, asking for a remedy. Her present husband was impotent and she was a full, beautiful woman in the prime of her life. Why? Why was she in such a tragic situation? She went on to say that there was this other man she knew and she wondered if she could have an affair with him and remain with her husband because she did love her husband; she simply wanted to fulfill all of her womanhood. Cayce responded by showing just why she was in such a predicament. In a past incarnation during the Crusades, she and her present husband were also married to each other. He was then one of the greatest of the Crusaders, going off to the wars often. However, every time he left he put her under lock and key, even to the point of a chastity belt! She swore deep in her heart she would get even with him. Now she had him right where she always wanted him, and she could make him pay dearly.

What a triangle! I wouldn't be surprised if the other man had also been hanging around the castle while the men were off to the wars. But here they all were, set-up so neatly for a resolution to their past actions with each other. The husband had used his free will to squash his wife's, forcing her to submit to his will without any choice on her part. Now he found himself subjected to her will and her choices. She now had the power and weapons to make him pay. She found herself torn by her vow of revenge and her desire to simply enjoy her physical beauty and youth. Unfortunately, she also found herself wanting to make a success of her marriage and her home, and despite his past wrong, she loved her husband and he returned that love. What a tangled web. The choice was completely hers. There was now nothing standing in her way. Cayce advised her to do whatever she would want done to her, and she did. She withdrew from the other man's affections and built a loving home with her husband. No doubt she will eventually incarnate into a life filled with physical, mental, emotional and spiritual happiness and the rest of the world will probably look at her and think she is just lucky.

Relationships, of course, are not just within a family. One example of how the past lives of our soul can affect us in other relationships is that of a business man who happened to get many readings from Edgar Cayce. These readings revealed just how complex a typical business meeting can be when the soul's experiences are included. When Walter Morrison walked into a board meeting, he was walking into a history that reached far beyond his present life. Amid the members of this board were souls who had been his conquerors, his servants, his concubines, his cohorts and even his bitter enemies! Imagine what the underlying motivations were when Walter made a proposal which the group had to vote on, or when Walter had to cast his vote concerning a proposal by one of the other members of this band of souls. Who among the group would tend to support him? Who would tend to thwart his efforts and ideas? And who would he tend to support and resist? Many of the answers lie in their past-life experiences with each other on a soul level, experiences that they would innately respond to through their affinities and antipathies for one another. Walter himself was curiously amazed at how well the past-life readings predicted his present feelings for various members of the board. Only in a few cases did he find he really didn't have any particular innate reaction to a member. In most cases, the members that consistently rubbed him the wrong way were those who had been on his bad side in past lives, and those that seemed to agree and support him consistently were those who had done so in the past.

When relationships are viewed with a past-life perspective, the dynamics of the behavior, including the attitudes and emotions, of a relationship become more than just current moodiness or general personality traits. There are undercurrents of memory that simply cannot be easily ignored. Before we look into how we can discover our past-lives, lets look at another example from the Cayce material, an example that gives us a view of many lifetimes. This example in the next chapter not only gives us many lifetimes but it also gives us a view into the overall soul-life and soul-history.

CHAPTER FOUR
THE LIVES OF LELA:
ONE SOUL'S JOURNEY

Since Lela Evans died when she was only two and a half, we might well expect there would be very little story to tell. Actually, the real story begins with this little girl's death. If she had lived, she would have been a close companion of Edgar Cayce, who incarnated seven short months after her death. The doctors never really knew exactly why Lela died. Her mother always felt she slowly drifted away because the family situation had become less than ideal for a little girl, particularly this little girl.

Lela died August 24, 1876. Some sixty years later, 1936, a woman walked into the offices of the then aging Edgar Cayce and asked if he would give her one of his now famous psychic readings. Mr. Cayce didn't need to give a reading to know who this woman was—he would have recognized the soul of Lela anywhere—but the reading served to confirm it, she was indeed the same soul he knew so well. The reading went on to say that Lela withdrew from that brief incarnation because the situation in the home was not what she had expected it to be. The reading intimates that the souls of Lela and her parents must have made an agreement with one another prior to the incarnation concerning the kind of home they would have together in their next earthly life. Lela's expectations must have been very specific and emotionally vital for her to leave a family who so adored her. The readings say she withdrew "to the deeper meditation in the Mercurian environs!"

This quoted comment refers to a frequently expressed concept in the Cayce readings concerning the soul's experiences between physical lifetimes as sojourns in the surrounding environments of our solar system, particularly in and near the other planets in our system. We don't actually live *on* the planets as we do in the third dimension, but rather within and about their fourth and fifth dimensional environs. It's as though each planet and star has its unique complex of experiences that attract and shape our attitudes and consciousness. Apparently, Lela withdrew to what we might call the consciousness-complex that is somehow related to the three-dimensional planet we call Mercury. Apparently, in the other dimensions Mercury is quite a different environ that we perceive with carnal eyes. It seems the astrologers have long known that the planets were more than physical spheres in dark space because they have assigned each of them a special set of characteristics and energies that influence us. Mercury has astrologically represented the mind and its forces. This is where Lela sojourned before returning to the environs and dimension of earth, subsequently incarnating as Barbara Murry.

The reading went on to point out that she sojourned

in the realms of Mercury for exactly one full cycle, 33 years, before returning to this planet and incarnating again on August 24, 1910. It further explained that she once again had had a childhood home setting that was less than she desired, forcing her to make a decision as to whether she would endure the shortcomings of this particular family in order to take advantage of the opportunities available through these parents and their home environment.

She was only thirty years old as she sat next to Edgar Cayce who was now in his sixties. She would have been about three years older than him had she stayed with her earlier family situation, but as it was she was in the prime of her life. There she sat, listening to his description of her soul's life that seemed to have been going on forever. Life is so amazing when viewed from the perspective of the soul. The reading told of her soul's life from the very beginning. The story went something like this:

Lela's soul was first conceived in the Mind of God, as were each of us. She was among the numerous lights that appeared in the dark, still Infinity when the "morning stars sang together in the heavens." It was the first dawn and she found herself awake and filled with wonder. In this early morning light her virgin consciousness would have been so near to the infinite, omnipotent mind of her Creator that the two were one. Throughout this wondrous Presence were countless others like herself, yet each with a slightly different point-of-being in the Whole.

What creatures these would have been, like no other. They possessed the ultimate combination of consciousness and freedom. Within them were the innate urges of their Creator's desire for companionship and creativity, two celestially primal drives that would remain a driving force within each of them forever.

The angels must have looked upon these cosmic-toddlers with justifiable apprehension. Like celestial children they would have to learn to handle and value the treasures of this angelic home with care, but until they did learn what would the heavens be like? Chaos was a very real potential! It must have quickly become apparent to the angels that their home would never be the same again.

Flush with life, their minds ablaze with wonder and imbued with the essence of their Creator, these fledgling gods began to move, to touch, to seek out and look through the seemingly endless fathoms of the Cosmos. As a child would explore everything she found before her, Lela and the others peered into the different mansions of their Father's house. Wonders upon wonders were to be found everywhere their young minds turned.

As with so many of us, Lela's wonder brought her into the environs of our present solar system. When she fully arrived here the earth was still cooling and life was just beginning to stir in its waters and gases. This first appearance was not an incarnation of Lela's for there were no earthly bodies as we know them today. In this dawn of Earth's life she was more like a spirit in the breeze, a voice in the wind as it swept across the steaming waters—a voice foretelling of the coming of man.

Earth was not the only planet she visited. All the planets in this star system provided her with unique perspectives and opportunities in her young life. Neither was the third-dimension her primary level of consciousness. In this childhood of the Sons and Daughters of God the entire universe with all its dimensions would have been theirs to enjoy. By doing so, each would grow in understanding and come to be a true companion to the One who created it.

Lela's soul was not alone. She was among countless souls that turned their attention on this little part of the universe.

At this point in her celestial life, Lela was not a female spirit. Like all the other companions, she possessed both sexual forces. She was male and female, androgenous. Her nature or "form" could best be described as a consciousness, which could, in moments, be very defined and unique, focusing-in on the minutest parts of manifested life, and at other moments could expand into the Universal Consciousness and perceive the Whole of Life. She was a microcosm of the Whole, a miniature of her Creator, a "chip off the old block." However, her experiences, feelings, memories, attitudes and developing opinions and desires created a uniqueness, what we would call her soul. If we approached her, we would see how life was being expressed, perceived and experienced by this one point in the Whole.

This was Lela in the heavens, long before she made a home in the earth plane.

On one of her early visits to Earth, she and the group of souls with whom she was traveling saw a strangely different quality in many of the souls who had been sojourning in the environs of Earth. They appeared to be changing. They were more dense and heavy and their consciousness seemed narrower, less universal. As she and her companions studied this phenomenon they realized that the other souls were gradually moving so deeply into the Earth's dimension that they were separating from the rest of life, taking on the shapes and dimensions of this new world. This was causing them to lose awareness of the other dimensions and the higher, finer aspects of their own being. They were no longer visiting this world, they were actually becoming part of it. Some of the souls she observed were actually beginning to look like the animals indigenous to Earth. They had feathers, scales, horns and other appendages of the animal forms that inhabited the earth. They were totally new creatures—terrestrial, heavy and very difficult to communicate with.

To her amazement, they had developed a hierarchy among themselves, setting some souls above others, something that was totally alien to them in the heavenly spheres where they were all children of the same family and parentage, equals.

Perhaps the most astonishing change was that the souls who were now leading these terrestrial groups were expounding a belief that there actually was no central, universal consciousness to remain attuned to, that in fact, their source of life was not a celestial Creator of love and joy, but simply the impersonal force of organic, material life. Each soul ws encouraged to take what it wanted from life, with little regard for others and no regard for the Whole of Life. Successful survivors deserved to live above and even upon the others because it would improve the race. Power, superiority, force, strength and survival of the fittest were among their many new beliefs.

Lela and her companions knew this was nonsense.

Some great distortion of perception had come over these souls and they needed to regain their finer nature and form in order to see the truth again. However, in order for Lela and her group to reach them, they were going to have to move deeper into the Earth's dimensions, a move very few of them wanted to make. However, they couldn't just leave these lost souls in such a ridiculous state of awareness. After much reflection, she and her companions felt sure they could maintain their spiritual consciousness while communicating with these terrestrial ones.

The plan was to approach those who were the least affected by the Earth's physical dimension, re-awaken them to the truth and then get them to convey to the others that they were heading in the wrong direction and needed to turn around and return to the higher dimensions of life and consciousness.

Though Lela had visited Earth before, this was to be her first sojourn among its unique realms. However, she was not in a body like the ones we occupy today. She, and those who came with her, made themselves known to the terrestrial souls by projecting three-dimensional images of themselves into the Earth's dimension using light, much in the wasy we create a holograph. At first Lela's image was much like a sphere of illuminated consciousness from which her thoughts could be conveyed to the terrestrial souls. When it became apparent that the terrestrial souls were too three-dimensionally focused to relate to these images, Lela and her companions began to project a form that approached the shape of our bodies today, only it was much lighter and less dense, still very much like a holographic image formed by light but with increasing definition.

Using this image she began to sojourn in what was to become the continent of Atlantis. Here many souls were living in various degrees of solidity and awareness. Since Lela retained her attunement to the Universal Consciousness, she was considered to be a goddess, a priestess. Many came to her for guidance and help in understanding what was happening to them and their companions, but she also met with strong, aggressive challenges from the leaders of the terrestrially bound souls. They challenged everything she and her companions held to be true about the Universal One, the higher dimensions and our true purposes for being.

It quickly became apparent that this transformation in consciousness was going to take much longer than originally expected. The terrestrially possessed companions were far more involved in this world than had first been suspected. In fact, many of them were actually seeking to build colonies here and sojourn among the planet's trees, mountains, waters and skies indefinitely. This might have been completely compatible with the Creator if they had not also been developing an almost idolic interest in themselves and their own desires without any regard for how they affected others and the Universe.

This self-seeking energy would prove to be the first evil, the first sin, and the followers and supporters of this self-centered movement would become known as The Children of Darkenss because their paths led toward the abyss of separation and loss of contact with the Creator. Prior to these changes there had been only the One Force. Now there were two and the second one was evil because, as it mounted life for its own purposes it destroyed everything in its way. The loss of contact with any holistic source and interconnection to all of life combined with the new paradigm reflected in the principles of "survival of the fittest," established an entirely new and inherently destructive dimension of consciousness.

Unfortunately, self-seeking was not the sole possession of the terrestrially bound souls. Every free-willed companion had within it the potential to begin seeking its own way without concern for the effect on others and the Whole. Free will and independent consciousness were godly gifts, yet with just the slightest shift in intent these sublime wonders of the fledgling gods became weapons of devils. Each of the companions had to struggle to subdue their self-only desires in order to remain in harmony with the Whole and the other companions.

Lela struggled hard to maintain her attunement and to aid those who sought her guidance and counsel, but she could feel herself assuming more and more of the substance of the earth, becoming heavier and, as she battled with the terrestrial leaders, she found herself becoming more willful and determined to force her views upon them. This righteous and well-meaning desire was subtly giving strength to forces of self-interest, but unlike some of her fellow companions, Lela perceived the effects of willfulness and resisted.

Her name was now Asamee. Hers was not exactly an individual name as we have today, rather, it was the name of a line of souls all of whom were called, "Asamee." Individualness was not near what it has become today. Differentiating one soul from another wasn't done; all were still very much one. Those who felt as she did about life and consciousness were being called "The Children of the Law of One." This name came to them because of their insistence that there was only one force in the universe and the souls were the children of this One. They also taught "The Law of the One," which included a principle that actions naturally produce reactions, an idea that the terrestrial ones considered ridiculous and just another way to keep them from doing whatever they wanted.

According to the Cayce readings, one of the souls who was Asamee in these times was called, Amilius. This soul would later become known as Jesus of Nazareth, savior of the world. His story weaves in and out of Lela's and is a fascinating one in itself. Cayce said that in these very early times on the planet, Amilius perceived the disastrous change that had come over his fellow souls, resulting in the terrestrial ones, and perceiving this change he came to the conclusion that things had gotten beyond the level of a brief flirtation with the earth. It was now time to develop a much more long-term plan for dealing with the situation. On this point, many of the Children of the Law of One disagreed or had other ideas about how better to deal with the problem. Thus, for the first time, a difference of opinion arose within the ranks of the Children. Nevertheless, Amilius was certainly attuned to the Universal Consciousness, his intentions pure and his vision clear. Because of this, most of the Children supported his perceptions, some begrudgingly, others wholeheartedly, and of course, some resisted them strongly.

Amilius perceived that if this loss of celestial

consciousness could happen to one soul, it could happen to any soul and, therefore, the problem needed to be faced; the temptation needed to be overcome, not avoided. Furthermore, the root of the problem was not the Earth and its unique form of life, but the struggle within each soul to learn to use its godliness in such a way as to be all it was meant to be and yet not destroy itself and other life in the process. Key to this problem was the sense of separation that a soul felt as it became more self-conscious and less universally conscious. This sense of separation, which resulted in a loss of purpose and identity with anything or anyone, occurred in the celestial realms as well as in the Earth, but it was more accentuated in the Earth's dimension. Therefore, perhaps this world, the Earth, was the best place to conquer it.

Amilius was making a commitment to enter the earth and live among the lost ones and somehow overcome its destructive influences. He believed if self-consciousness and its resulting sense of separation could be overcome, it could be overcome here as well as anywhere else, and once it was overcome it would no longer have any power over the children, the future companions of God. They would know the truth and they would be free.

Some among Amilius' group wanted to leave these earthlings to wallow in their own sins and delusions. Others doubted their own ability to resist the temptations that had so possessed the lost souls. In addition to dealing with this problem of one's own inner temptations and struggles, they were going to have to deal with the terrestial souls who had now become very aggressive and lawless. To attempt to live among them was not only spiritually, mentally and emotionally dangerous, it was physically dangerous. Some of the Children also pointed out that there were many complications involved in this Earth problem, so many complexities and complications that a real solution might well be impossible, and that they would just be throwing good souls after bad if they attempted to enter and subdue this world.

With all of these hazards in mind and in spite of much bickering among the Children, Lela, then called Asamee, and her fellow souls, including Amelius, began to set up a system whereby the lost ones could regain their heavenly consciousness and, along with the Children of the Law of One, learn to overcome their potential for evil. It was a grand endeavor, filled with that spirit that is only found in the faithful, the hopeful, the positive ones. Little did they know just how formidable their adversary was, both the inner and outer.

First on their list was to prepare a physical form that would allow the companions of God to sojourn in the Earth with some semblance of their true, spiritual nature. The forms being used by the terrestrial ones were totally wrong for their true nature and actually added to their problems with perception and understanding. Since these were the companions of the Creator, they needed a physical form that suited their particular characteristics and yet functioned well in the third-dimension. The terrestrial ones were manifesting animal-like appearances and bodies. These would have to be changed and a totally new form created, yet it would have to be based on the same principles which caused the animal forms to function well in the Earth, with its time and space and three dimensions.

Furthermore, the lost ones showed every indication of having separated their sexual parts. No longer were they androgenous. They were now either predominantly masculine or feminine in their appearance and energy. The natural duality of this planet seemed to have caused them to accentuate one of their sexual forces and subdue the other. Therefore, the new, single-sexed bodies would have to reflect the different aspects of the two sexes. Asamee and her fellow "double-sexed" companions began the work of creating forms for the souls, male and female forms, and separating their double-sexed natures into single-sexed physical projections. Amilius was the first to completely achieve this.

All of these struggles and the subsequent commitment and work occurred in Atlantis. Many souls were involved, and Lela interacted with most of them. Throughout her incarnations these souls would weave in and out of her life. In some cases, they built strong, lasting relationships that were always a blessing to them. In other cases, they built disagreements, misunderstandings and distrust that haunted them whenever their paths crossed.

As this work continued, Lela withdrew from the Earth to prepare herself to be a channel through which the Children could enter into the new human bodies. She chose to accentuate her feminine forces and subdue her masculine, and throughout her many incarnations never changed her mind, remaining female in each.

These early periods in the Earth had gone on for an

enormously long time. In Earth time, the activities in Atlantis lasted some 200,000 years. During the last 50,000 years the huge continent had been broken into several islands by violent earthquakes. Lela had sojourned here as Asamee for much of the early period and was preparing to return to Earth as the last of Atlantis sank into the sea and a new era began.

This would be her first true incarnation in that she was actually going to enter and live in a physical body, a female body, for the first time. It was not a haphazard event. Many of the souls with whom she had worked in Atlantis were already in the Earth preparing for her incarnation.

Conditions in the Earth had changed dramatically. En masse the souls had entered, preparing for generations of incarnations that were to be a part of this new world, this new experience, which would hopefully end joyfully.

In five different regions, in five different races, in five different nations the souls entered, each group manifesting a unique characteristic of their celestial nature and each responsible for maintaining and enlightening the physical world with that celestial aspect while the cycles of Earth-life moved toward their destiny.

Lela was among those souls charged with developing a white race. Its original center was in the Caucasus Mountains, though many of them migrated into what today would be called northern Africa, Egypt and eastern Asia and Europe.

In Egypt, the priest Ra Ta and several others working closely with him were preparing for Lela's entry. Hers was to be a very special event for she had the potential to manifest all the best characteristics of a true, pure human-type physical body. Many of the bodies in all the races were contaminated and distorted by animal characteristics that lingered from the early days of the terrestrial ones. To produce a perfect form for the companions, one had to use the natural laws of the earth's genetics combined with a clear mental image of what it was they were trying to achieve and then hope the soul that inhabited the body possessed the same image and could maintain it long enough to manifest firmly in physical form. Even then, they could end up sexually mingling with another body that wasn't as purely human, mixing it with stronger animal characteristics, and ruin everything. These were un-usual times. There were no families, no parents, no laws, just millions and millions of souls in different degrees of consciousness, different motives and desires, and different physical bodies. The celestially attuned companions were living in human-like terres-trial forms, and though this proximity helped awaken many of the lost ones, it also helped to lower the awarenesses of the celestial ones.

Despite the temptations and difficulties, Ra Ta and his co-workers had prepared themselves and their bodies carefully. Among themselves they had selected two who were genetically, as well as mentally and spiritually, the best. These had been developed, pre-served and finally brought together for the conception of a third body, and hopefully, this channel would be even better than the parent bodies.

Lela had also prepared herself well. She had sojourned in the celestial environs with as pure an attunement to the Universal One as she could possibly manage. Her attunement was not like it had once been in the early morning moments after the original creation, when her life and awareness were one with All life—too much had come between her and the deep stillness of the Universal One—but it was an attunement sufficient enough to make her a rare soul among earth-bound souls and to bring a glimpse to others of what it had been like to be a morning star in that now distant dawn.

Ra Ta anxiously watched as the new born was being received from the womb, and as it was being cleaned and prepared for presentation. His eyes searched for the tell-tale signs of beastliness or celestialness and the true characteristics of a pure human form. Again and again he scanned every detail of her body. Nothing, absolutely nothing was distorted or contaminated. She was truly human. Clear sharp eyes, pure skin, very little hair—the priest could hardly believe his eyes. She was the perfect human form for the heavenly souls to use during their incarnations in this new world. As he pulled away to reflect on the meaning and potential of this event, the others with him pushed their way in to see for themselves.

The celestially aware companions entered in five different races. This was originally accomplished more in consciousness than in form. Their bodies did not immediately reflect true, pure human qualities but had to be developed toward this aim. At this early stage in man's entry into the Earth, human qualities were more mental images than physical forms, and in order to convert these into physical forms they would have to work within the evolutionary and genetic laws native to this world.

Ra Ta and his companions had finally achieved the white body. The red had already been perfected, as well as the black, and the brown and yellow were also near completion. Lela had been the soul that entered this first purely caucasian body. Her new name was Tar Ello, "body of light." It was a high achievement for Lela. She gave hope and inspiration to many through her beautiful reflection of one of the five aspects of the heavenly "form." Man was no longer a beast of the world, but a descendant from another world above, a beautiful descendant. Now the work of the ascension was ahead of them, the return to their life "before the world was."

Though Lela, Tar Ello, had accomplished much in achieving her first flesh body, it would prove to be a very difficult incarnation for her. She was looked upon with awe and reverence, and viewed and judged by her outer form more than her inner spirit. She naturally felt special, different and more alone than she had ever felt in the higher dimensions. Even some of her closest companions in the spirit were now so in awe of her that they set her above themselves, no longer swapping council and support with her but expecting all the wisdom and strength to come from her. Others, who had been her friends and colleagues in the Atlantian sojourn, now resented her new physical superiority, feeling that she no more deserved such an honor than they did.

Lela longed for the early times when no soul was greater than another and all shared with each other as equals and companions. Here everything was measured and judged by appearance, position and power. It was a lonely place to live, each within their own body, separated from the others and measured by their outer qualities and segregated accordingly.

Ra Ta perceived the girl's sadness, though ever so subtle it was, for she kept her mission above her personal needs. He encouraged her to take part in the ceremonies of the temples and find comfort in prayer and meditation. Ax-Tell and his son Ax-Tellus, both remnants of the Atlantian civilization and members of the perfected red race, had long understood the problems of loneliness and separation in this new world. Seeing this same feeling in the eyes of this little white child and in so many others, they encouraged the priest and the king of the land to consider a new living arrangement for souls while incarnate in the Earth. Instead of living in medium to large groups, each group would break into small sub-groups consisting of one male and one female whose offspring lived with them. Together they would form a support group for each of their members. The bonding force would be their own flesh and blood. It was the beginning of the family and the sense of support that came from being someone's child, brother or sister, or parent. This structure would also reflect the heavenly realms where the children of the father-mother God companioned in a close, nurturing environment.

It was an excellent idea but Tar Ello belonged to the temple virgins and there was no way Ra Ta was going to agree to allow her to live in a separate dwelling with her natural parents amid all the other souls of mixed blood and morality. This world was still too savage and beastly for that. She was too rare, too special. But those close to Tar Ello knew she carried a deep sadness and loneliness with her and she would not be the perfect temple priestess Ra Ta wanted. Nevertheless, she struggled hard to maintain her attunement to the Universal One and carried out her daily work to the best of her ability.

She continued to help make flesh a temporary home for spirit, drawing inspiration and guidance from her temple studies and duties and the many teachers and guides associated with the effort. One of these guides was Hermes, called by many the "Thrice Majestic One." He was, in fact, the soul who had been called Amilius in Atlantis. Continuing his work toward resurrecting the earth-bound souls to their former state in the heavens, he was now here in Ancient Egypt among the many other Children who also worked toward such an end. As it is commonly known among the mystery students of today, Hermes was the major influence in the building of the Pyramids. Since the descent of the souls was going to take them deep into the world of matter and physical reality these monuments were built as reminders of the former realms that still lie beyond physical death. But they were more than monuments in those early days. Lela and her fellow Children of the One used some of these structures for their initiations into the true realities and purposes for life, truths that were fast becoming myths and legends instead of realities.

Through her close relationship with the priest Ra Ta and his close relationship with Hermes, she continued to be involved with this great soul and His destiny.

Unfortunately, after the death of the priest, who had become her inspiration and strength, Tar Ello fell from the high pedestal she had so unwittingly accepted. Eventually, she left the temple and joined with

Exderenemus, another remnant of Atlantis, as a companion. The soul of Exderenemus would be her companion in many of her Earth incarnations.

These dramatic changes in Tar Ello's life and position astonished those who worshipped her and caused those who resented her to take every opportunity to discredit her. All of this left Lela's soul deeply distressed. What had begun as a grand endeavor was ending in a purposeless mess. She withdrew from her body, from this place of sadness, and sought to rid herself of the memory of the whole experience. Higher and higher her spirit rose until she could feel the light of the Universal One fill her being and purge her of her earthly dross, leaving it to die. Here in the heavenly spheres she bathed and rejuvenated herself until once again she and her Creator were in touch with each other.

As Earth keeps time, it wasn't long before the soul of the priest and Lela's other companions beckoned her to join them in another visit to the environs of Earth and another attempt at overcoming its peculiar influences while helping the terrestrially bound souls reawaken themselves. It was too much a part of Lela's deepest wishes for her to refuse this goodwill mission, and since the Earth afforded her the opportunity to mend her disappointing sojourn in Egypt, she readily accepted the challenge. Off she went, revitalized and ready to make all aright.

Together with her little band of like-minded souls, Lela lived through many, many different lifetimes in the Earth and in the realms between Earth lifetimes, as well. Members of this loose-knit band were not always in agreement with each other or even nice to each other, but, for that matter, as is so often true of families, they were a unit, even at times, a team. One of their most significant incarnations came during the time of Christ.

In this incarnation Lela and Ra Ta were brother and sister. Her name was Nimmuo and his was Lucius. Both were prominent members of the church at Laodicea. The setting, as many of us know, was the Holy Land during the occupation of the Roman Legions. That particular portion of Asia had been under the control and supervision of the Roman Empire for a very long time. Their presence and power permeated every aspect of life in these regions.

Nimmuo's father was of Roman descent and had two wives, one Grecian and one Jewish. Nimmuo was the child of the Greek mother while her brother, Lucius, was the son of the Jewish mother. Since the Romans always made attempts to put in authority any locals who showed the potential for having sympathy with the needs and demands of the Empire, or who could be helpful in making activities with the local people more harmonious, her Roman born father and therefore, she and her family, enjoyed the support of Rome. The armies of Rome did not want trouble with the people it conquered. For very practical reasons, they simply couldn't afford to keep expending any more of their resources governing these distant lands. Because of these practical needs and their policy of working with and supporting any locals who showed signs of peaceful co-existence with them, Nimmuo's family was given many financial and personal freedoms that were rare in those times. Her father, with his Jewish wife and close connections with the Jewish churches in the

North, was considered to be of great benefit to the Empire as a friend, and so his family and even their Jewish church enjoyed the powerful support of Rome. Nevertheless, Nimmuo and her family held tightly to the tenets and morals of their Hebrew faith, and though they interacted with the Roman leaders, avoided much of the lewdness and immorality that they brought to the Holy Land.

As the activities and teachings of Jesus reached their homeland in the north, the family began to come under the influence of these teachings. To these souls of the Children of the Law of One, Jesus' teachings were a balm to their weary souls and a beacon pointing the way to a forgotten consciousness and life. However, when the changes began to occur during the periods of the trial, the Crucifixion, and then the subsequent reports that spread across the land as to what actually happened in the last hour of the Crucifixion, the reports of His rising again three days later and meeting with the disciples at the Sea of Tiberius, the entire family was caught up in wonderment and interest.

So Nimmuo, then barely sixteen years old, and her brother, who was now a leading minister in their church, set off to the south to learn everything they could about these reports. Nimmuo wanted to meet and talk with everyone who had come in contact with the Master.

Because she and her brother traveled under the protection and support of the Romans, many along the way were skeptical of their true faith and loyalty to Israel and the Master's teachings. However, the sincerity and faithfulness of these two northerners was genuine and quickly perceived by the people they visited who shared with them the many stories about the Master's life and teachings.

They journeyed through the Holy Land, across the Sea of Galilee, down to those lands in Jordan, through Perea to Bethany and the house of Martha, Mary and Lazarus, and then into the city of Jerusalem itself. They met Mary the Mother of Jesus and the rest of the family that had gathered under John's roof as he had been instructed from the Cross.

In Bethany they heard the story about Mary Magdalene's cleansing from her sins and Martha's devotion and tireless efforts to care for everyone's needs. Straight from Lazarus himself they heard about his death and his feelings and consciousness during the four days that his dead body lay in the tomb, and what it was like in the realms between Earth-life and Spirit-life, and how he heard and felt the movement within himself when the Voice called, "Lazarus, come forth!"

All this affected Nimmuo to her very soul, making some contact with those old sensations when she had been so close to her Creator. These feelings and stories would become a part of her soul-memory forever.

She listened to the reports of how people had been healed by the laying on of His hands or merely His word spoken, how they had eaten bread that had been created by the word of the Teacher. She and her brother were forever changed by the experience. Over and over they heard the many accounts of what had happened. This first-hand hearing by Nimmuo and Lucius was very important to the others in their church in the north because the reports they had been receiving had been translated through many tongues before reaching them and much had been lost in the process. Now, Nimmuo and Lucius would be able to take these reports back to their family, friends and church members in Laodicea in great detail.

However, these times of enlightenment and awakening were not to pass peacefully. The Romans began to move against this growing new group of inspired trouble-makers and their teachings and followers. Nimmuo was present at one such event when James, the brother of Jesus, was chosen as head of the new church along with Peter. She witnessed how the other James and his brother John, the sons of Zebedee, had so stirred the spirit of the crowds that the Romans became afraid of the mass meeting and attacked with the swords drawn, killing John's brother and many others during the riot and eventually exiling John to Patmos. These two sons of Zebedee had long been called the sons of thunder and the Romans had had enough of them and their friends. From this moment on the followers of the humble Nazarene would be persecuted by the authorities.

With the scattering of the disciples and friends, Nimmuo and her brother returned to Laodicea and the other churches of the north. Here they both grew in power and position because of their travels and the things they knew and understood about this great event. Deep within Nimmuo she felt the essence of those things she heard in the homes of Mary, Martha, Lazarus and the Mother. As so often in her previous lives, her soul yearned for the Spirit, for that soothing sense of the Divine Presence that she had always loved. Now, amid all the daily activities of this world and its limited perspective on life, she applied herself to the work that had begun many thousands of years earlier in that lost and forgotten land of Atlantis.

Everyone around her in this life had been involved with her in Atlantis and Egypt, and several lifetimes in between. Amilius, that soul who had been so attuned in the early periods that he committed himself to the rescue of the lost souls, was the very person they now called, "Jesus." In this Divine incarnation He prepared the final phase of salvation for all earth-bound souls. He and the heavenly Father were one throughout this life, not separate. This showed to all who could still see with their spiritual, celestial eyes that it could be done, thereby making it easier for others to do also. His words came from beyond this present world, from the Universal Consciousness, our heavenly Father who created us in the very beginning:

"You are not of this world" (John 3:12)

"Is it not written in your laws that you are gods? Yet you say... 'Thou blasphemest' because I say I am the Son of God." (John 10: 34-36)

"In my Father's house are many mansions... I go to prepare a place for you...And where I go you know, and you know the way." (John 14:2 & 4)

"I came forth from the Father and came into the world, now I leave the world and go to the Father." (John 16:28)

"No man has ascended up to heaven but he that came down from heaven..." (John 3:13)

These words and the stories she heard on her journey through Jesus' homelands filled Lela, now Nimmuo, with a new fervor and determination to continue with the work. Along with her brother and many others, she ministered to the needs of the people, particularly those involved in the church at Laodicea. And when the church was nearly destroyed from within by a severe difference of opinion on how best to judge what was right and what was wrong, Nimmuo's serene and patient council kept the church from dividing in two. She seemed to sense the inner meaning of the teachings and never got lost in the many surface interpretations and dogmas that man always tried to build and then bind others to.

This was not an easy time for Lela. She was surrounded by the very same souls who had seen her fall in Egypt, and many of them doubted her new-found inspiration and suspected she would once again let them down. But they underestimated her determination to make things right with all those souls she had once failed. This was her opportunity and she seized it, snatching victory from out of the mouth of defeat. This was Lela's finest hour. With all the wisdom and strength within her, she rose to the occasion and many other souls rose a little higher because of her.

She lived a long and fulfilling life and withdrew to the peace of the heavenly environs for a lengthy period of meditation, letting the truths of that incarnation permeate deeply into her consciousness. She was a far wiser child of God than the one who taught in Atlantis. She had seen the face of the beast and tamed it, at least most of it; there was a little more yet to deal with, as she would soon see.

After sojourning in the heavens for many earth-years, she returned for an incarnation that was most uncharacteristic of Lela. The earth was now a major center of physical activity and densely populated. All of life and the universe was now viewed almost totally from a physical perspective. Earth history established and supported the concept of physical reality being the only certain reality, and nearly everyone lived by this guiding concept. Business and commerce, religion and government, love and money had all become the powerful structures in which most lived. Into this world, so very different from that earlier world, Lela incarnated as one of the daughters of a wealthy and prominent Englishman. Her name was Marge Olglethorp. She learned her role well and even enjoyed it. Parasols, long, whirling hoop skirts and fancy buggies and parties with all kinds of foods and beverages were the style of the day. Life was just a bowl of cherries, ripe for the eating and enjoying. Amazingly, Lela, as Marge, took to this little fun lifetime quite well. No great mission beyond pomp and pleasure, no great challenges to overcome beyond style and good taste—life was to be lived to its fullest.

On one of the family's journeys to America, Marge found herself caught-up in the life of a southern belle and was well received by the ladies and gentlemen of this land of willows and moss, huge plantations and wealth beyond measure. Here she lived the life of a Georgia peach, with that special touch of breeding that is forever English. Ra Ta was not involved in this lifetime, but Exderenemus, her husband in Ancient Egypt, was. In fact, he had incarnated with her in the Palestine lifetime when she was Nimmuo, but the two of them did not develop a very close relationship in that life. However, in this present incarnation in England and Southern America a terrible disagreement ended their relationship with such bitterness that they would of necessity face it again in a future incarnation.

How did this carefree lifetime become part of the experience of a soul who was once the goddess of Atlantis, the perfection of Ancient Egypt and a minister of Laodicea? The Eastern teachings of reincarnation include a concept that souls live a carefree incarnation about every six incarnations, a vacation, if you will, from the main work of spiritual resurrection. Perhaps Lela was enjoying a much needed break from her many serious lifetimes of devotion, trial and hard lessons learned.

After her incarnation as Marge, she reincarnated as Lela Evans only to withdraw in two and a half years for the environs of Mercury. She then reincarnated as Barbara Murry and eventually ended up sitting next to the "sleeping prophet" Edgar Cayce, as he had been called in one biography. Barbara was a serene, elegant woman who devoted much of her time and energy to the work of Edgar Cayce, who, not surprisingly, was the reincarnation of the soul who had been Ra Ta in Ancient Egypt. In this present lifetime, Barbara married Exderenemus again, now called Ryan Simons. The Cayce reading warned them not to let this relationship end like it had in the previous life. Amilius was now their Christ, having become one with the Father again and resurrected to prepare a place for them and each and everyone of us. The three of them dedicated themselves and their lives to this soul they had known so closely throughout His lifetimes and His earthly mission. They continued to live and teach the mystery that we are all celestial beings descended from our original kingdom through a long and hard journey in this realm of physical reality and destined to return from whence we came.

In looking over this story of Lela, the view that all the world is a stage and every person but an actor playing a role becomes a strong image for what is actually occurring. Lela's soul, and every soul, takes on the role and personage of a certain character and through this part experiences what it is like to be the character. This is not just assuming the features and activities of the character, but actually experiencing life from its perspective. Surrounded in the thoughts, emotions and attitudes that are a part of this unique role, the soul gains an understanding of consciousness and life. Through this process the soul begins to discover the nature of life as a Whole and him or herself as an individual within that Whole. One matures and grows wiser and more clear about one's purposes and lasting needs and desires. The Earth, in this way, is a large stage upon which celestial companions of God play out their fantasies, learning what life is really like and what is truly enduring and valuable.

PART TWO

THE PRESENT AND FUTURE

CHAPTER FIVE
HOW TO REMEMBER
YOUR PAST LIVES

Let's approach this subject by first developing some insights into the nature of life on the earth plane. Then we'll look at the various levels of consciousness and how they relate to life here. Finally, we'll look at the techniques commonly used to discover our soul's memories.

The fact that the conscious mind does not remember any previous lives shows us that past lives and their memories do not belong to the conscious part of our being but to a much deeper part of us. Our outer selves are truly fresh, new projections from out of our deep, older, inner selves.

I think the metaphor of the actor playing a role and the actor as a person is a good one. In some ways, our personality, conscious mind and physical bodies (in other words, our outer, conscious selves) are the actor's role and costume. The script is written by the forces of the Law of Cause and Effect. The stage and set-design (conditions in our life) contribute to the unfolding of the story and its plot which are all set up for this one performance (the earth life). Our souls, as individuals, assume their respective roles by donning the character they are to play (personality) and their costume (body) and then taking their place on the stage (the conditions in life). In this metaphor, the role and the story are played out to a denouement that is not predetermined by the script. Though the roles and the story strongly set the direction of the play, they do not predetermine the ending; it is allowed to unfold as the characters play their parts. Finally, the characters and costumes are discarded and the actors leave the stage to return to their real lives (soul lives). But, as we know, they will come again and don new costumes, assume new roles and a new story will be played out.

Whether we perceive it or not, past-life experiences and memories, or the roles our souls have played before, are affecting our present lives at this very moment. These past experiences affect us in two arenas. The first is comprised of our present *outer* world with the circumstances and conditions before us each day (the stage and setting of our life). The second is comprised of our *inner* world of personal consciousness, comprised of our innate inner nature (a combination of the actor as a person and the actor's assumed character in the role).

The outer arena would include the opportunities and limitations of our families, neighborhoods, countries and the world during our lifetime. The outer arena presents each of us with a different stage and setting upon which to play our part. Some of us are born into loving, supportive families, while others are born into no family at all. Some of us are born into lands of poverty, famine and war, while others are born into lands of opportunity, abundance and peace. Some of us incarnate during times of great struggles in the world, while others come during times of great peace and prosperity, etc. How often have we heard one generation say of another, "They never knew the hardships we had to live through." And because they didn't, their outer arena was very different from the other generation, and therefore, life was very different for each. The outer arena presents us with unique circumstances and conditions within which we will live our lives.

Along with these outer influences, we are born with a unique inner arena of personal consciousness. This consists of our innate temperaments, dispositions, attitudes, emotions and mental abilities. It also includes our physical health and innate self-image. The world behind our eyes possesses much of its nature *before* we even begin to live this life. Hence, a newborn baby expresses its unique temperament and disposition within moments after birth, and the mother can quickly recognize the difference from her other babies. Then, as we live and experience life, this inner arena is further developed and changed by our environment, or the events and forces in our outer arena. But two people can have the same set of outer circumstances in their lives and each will experience these circumstances in different ways because their innate inner arenas are different. One's emotional and mental nature affects how an outer situation will be perceived and experienced.

In Diagram "A", LEVELS OF CONSCIOUSNESS, we can get an idea of how these two arenas co-exist. At the very tip of the "V" in figure #1 is our body with its five physical senses. Beyond this is the outer arena of the physical world and our physical life. As we move within the Levels of Consciousness, we make a transition from outer-world to inner-world and toward the consciousness of our soul and its life. This inner-world begins with the Conscious Level which is most closely associated with the outer arena and in which our personality is developed. Then it continues upward to the Subconscious which has the unique position of being between the two realities of outer life and the very "deep" inner life that culminates in the broad expanse of our Superconscious and the Universal Mind. Our Superconscious is the highest level of individual awareness before merging into the nonindividualized Whole of the Universal Consciousness. At this level we know ourselves to be ourselves and yet one with the Whole.

In figure #2 of Diagram "A" we can see how two people relate to each other using this model of consciousness and the inner and outer arenas. In the outer arena they communicate with each other using the five physical senses. For example, one vibrates its vocal chords and this, in turn, vibrates the other's eardrums and they speak and hear each other. However, as they move within themselves there is another level at which they can and do communicate, the Superconscious Level. Here their communications do not require the physical body's senses: their thoughts are transferred directly, telepathically.

The present conditions in the two arenas are the direct result of our soul's past. We are the way we are and our surroundings are the way they are because of what our soul has done with itself and its life *before* this life. Very little occurs in our present life that was not fore-ordained by our soul's past actions, thoughts and experiences. The Universal Law of Cause of Effect continues to work its mysterious way through our lives, ever presenting to our souls the effects of past actions.

There is one major exception to this. Nothing, not fate nor karma, exceeds the power of a soul to use its God-given will to choose a new course, a new attitude, a new motivation, a new set of guidelines by which to make decisions and react to situations. But until we choose to exercise our free will in forging new directions, we continue to be carried along on the forces of fate, karma and destiny which have been cast in the waters of our life by past choices and experiences, and are sustained by laws of attraction and habit patterns which continue to move us in the same old directions. However, once we do begin to assume responsibility for the way our lives are, it will be some time before the effects of our past choices have been met and the effects of our new choices begin to make an impact on us. Therefore, it is important that we gain some understanding of who we have been and what we have done with our gifts of consciousness and free will.

Discovering Our Soul's Past

The memories of past lives are located in two places. First, the mind of each individual spirit-soul contains the memories of that soul's experiences from its first inception. Second, the Universal Mind contains the records of every thought, word and action that has

DIAGRAM "A"

LEVELS OF CONSCIOUSNESS

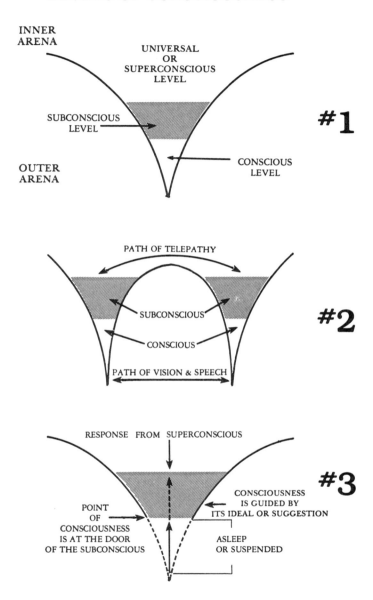

Dr. Herbert Bruce Puryear first introduced me to these diagrams. They are a result of his research and studies at the Association for Research and Enlightenment (A.R.E.).

occurred during the manifestation of life. This is often called, "The Akashic Record" or "Akasha" from a Sanskrit word referring to the essential substance of the Universe. It is believed that all thoughts and activities of manifested life make an impression on the Universal Mind, leaving a record of all that has occurred. Anyone who is willing to make the effort required can actually "read" this Akashic record. Therefore, in order to remember or, more accurately, gain access to the soul memories or Akashic records, we need to get in touch with one of these two sources: Our own soul's memory or the memory of the Universal Mind.

First, let's look at how we can get in touch with our soul's memory. This level of our consciousness is often associated with the deeper realms of the Subconscious Mind. Because of this, many people have tried to reach into the soul's distant past using techniques that breach the conscious mind's normally dominant position and gain access to the Subconscious. The most popular techniques for doing this include hypnotic age regression, guided imagery sessions and reveries.

Hypnotic Age Regression

Basically, hypnotic age regression consists of hypnotizing an individual, causing the conscious mind to become unconscious and the subconscious to gain a more prominently conscious state. Once the subconscious is contacted the hypnotist proceeds to guide the subject back through his or her life, stopping at different points along the way to establish a sense of time in the subject's life. Eventually, the subject is directed to go beyond his or her birth and verbalize what he is experiencing or seeing with his inner eye. The number of times this technique has produced past-life memories is amazing. There are literally thousands of records by hundreds of excellent hypnotists.

Looking at Diagram "A," figure #3, we can get some idea of how this occurs. Through a series of techniques which can be gathered from the hypnosis books listed in the appendix, the Conscious Level is suspended allowing it to surrender its position to the Subconscious. Then, with the individual's consciousness at the door of the Subconscious, the hypnotist gives the suggestion to begin regressing back in time, eventually beyond the recent birth into past lives. Apparently, the inner part of the person uses the body's vocal chords and ears without the conscious part of the person realizing it. Typically, the conscious mind and personality of the individual remember nothing of the entire regression. Where is the Conscious Mind? How can all of this occur without it even being slightly aware? It's very difficult to answer these questions. Again, it seems that our outer selves are only a portion of our total being, and that our inner selves are much more dynamic than we have previously believed.

Guided Imagery & Reverie

Guided imagery and reverie sessions are much the same as hypnotic age regressions except that the subject's conscious mind is allowed to remain conscious throughout the session. Consequently, the subject potentially remembers the session quite well.

Usually, a guided imagery or reverie session begins with an open awareness on the part of the guide and the subject about what is going to occur. The subject then closes his or her eyes and begins to settle into a submissive state, allowing the guide to direct the attention of the subject's "inner eye" or "mind's eye" through a series of scenes or movements that have the effect of loosening the hold on the present and guiding him or her toward the distant past. All of this is occurring *within* the subject's normal, outer self, and while the outer self is conscious.

There are many varying techniques for guided imagery but each of them tries to move the present consciousness toward an inner view of other vistas, past vistas that the soul has seen and recalls. Once these past images are in the mind's eye, the guide can move the subject to look more carefully at them and "see" the people and events going on around him. From these descriptions we gain a picture of the soul's past memories.

Sometimes, while deeply involved in a past-life scene, the subject will become emotionally excited by the events and people it sees, revealing their power and impact. Our outer selves seem to have a built-in barrier that protects us from the direct impact of our soul's past experiences, especially those that are harmful or so unpleasant as to ruin any chance of correcting these mistakes in the present. This should be kept in mind when attempting to discover our soul's past, for some of the memories are hidden for a very good reason and to bring them to the surface by force could prove disastrous, crushing the outer person under a burden that even his or her own soul was not ready to bear. The past needs to be investigated and awakened, but the other ego-personalities involved in these investigations (e.g., hypnotists, guides and subjects) must not assume they always know what's best, and need to allow the inner-soul to reveal its secrets in a manner that suits its purposes and timing.

As with the hypnotic regression technique, the guided imagery/reverie subject is eventually led back to the present through the same sequence of suggestions. In a reverie or guided imagery session, the subject will usually show signs of having been affected by the recall, occasionally deeply affected or even changed by the recollection and realization of their inner being and past experiences. They will also consciously remember much of what has occurred.

Psychic Readings

Another popular way of discovering an individual's past lives is through a "psychic reading." Apparently, some individuals possess an ability to "see" or "read" the past lives of others. It is uncertain as to how this is done. Presumably, a psychic is able to contact a person's soul-memory or the Universal Mind, the Akashic Record. Using Diagram "A," figure #3, we see that both the individual's Subconscious and Superconscious can be accessed. If we look at figure #2, we can see how one individual could contact another's Subconscious and Superconscious by going within their own consciousness to a level where they could move (in consciousness) to the other's point of consciousness. In this way, one can actually gain information about another person that the latter may not even be aware of because they are so focused in their outer consciousness that they have little or no contact with their inner consciousness.

There are many different forms of psychic readings. Some are given while the psychic person remains conscious; others give readings during unconscious trance-like states. Sometimes a photo of the subject is requested, or their name and address, sometimes their time of birth. Many times a conscious psychic will use some sort of device for focusing in on the subject to begin the reading, such as tarot cards, an astrology chart, a crystal, etc. The trance psychic, on the other hand, often uses an internal focusing device or process, such as a mantra, an image, a tone, etc. In some cases, trance psychics contact discarnate souls in the spirit realm on the assumption that the discarnate soul can somehow get the information better than incarnate souls. Again, it is presumed that they are in touch with the subject's Subconscious Mind or the Universal Mind.

Where our imagination ends and true past-life recall begins is difficult to say. There is no sure way to know whether the past life is imagined or true, other than to judge by how well it settles with the present individual's innate characteristics and life circumstances. In hypnotic cases, we know that the subconscious is so amenable to suggestions that even the slightest variation in the tone of the hypnotist's voice can give away his inclination and thereby prejudice the subject's Subconscious to respond in kind. In reveries and guided image sessions, the conscious mind is actually encouraged to imagine, making it very difficult to know when one is imagining and when there is past-life recall. I suggest the only way we can be sure is to be as honest about our reactions to the past life as possible. If there is simply no identification with the scenario, perhaps it is of no significance. However, I would also suggest that we never completely discard it because as our life continues we may begin to see how this suggested past-life recall may well have been part of our soul's experience.

Another way to protect ourselves from fantasy and imagination is to select the hypnotist or guide with care. We could read some of their cases, study some of their former clients. We need to use some common sense in choosing the person and the procedure we are subjecting ourselves to before we spend our money. However, there is another route we can go, and though this way also has some uncertainties associated with it, it does have some distinct advantages over the previous techniques that I've described.

Dreams & Self-Realization

Two other sources for past-life recall are dreams and self-realization. Unfortunately, these are two of the least appreciated methods used today. Rarely do we seek within our own selves for answers to ourselves. Nevertheless, our dreams and self-realizations have an added bonus in that they not only provide us with past-life information but they do so in a way that builds a closer relationship between our outer and inner selves, integrating the two separate parts of our being. This bridge between our two islands of consciousness is so vital to our eternal life that to seek knowledge of our spirit-soul any other way robs us of one of the greatest journeys we will ever take.

Dreams and self-realization are certainly more difficult and long-term methods for discovering our past lives and the past lives of those who share our lives, but they are, without a doubt, two of the best all-around methods. The eventual friendship that develops from this reintegration of our Conscious with our Subconscious, our body with our spirit, our personality with our soul is worth all the effort involved.

Looking at Diagram "A," figure 3, we see how sleep brings our consciousness to the door of the Subconscious Mind. In this way, dreams are the Conscious Mind's recollection of the Subconscious' activities during the deepest phases of the sleep period. If the Conscious Level recalls the dream, records it, studies it, discerns a meaning and, finally, *uses* the knowledge in its life, then the whole individual begins to reunite and life takes on new dimensions. Since the deeper levels of consciousness are not confined to the dimension of time and space as is the outer conscious level, the past, even the distant past, is not difficult to know. Here the soul's story can be found. In Chapter Three we saw how Michael Parks learned of his past incarnation in France during the reign of Louis XIV. If you recall, that life-time was revealed to him through a series of dreams, each giving a fragment of the whole picture. The following dream is another example of how a past life can be discovered through dreams.

"I woke up around two or three in the morning thinking someone had made a loud noise in my bedroom. As I looked around I saw that everything was quiet. Nothing had happened. Lying back onto my pillow I began to recall what I had been dreaming just before waking. The strong smell of horses, leather and sweat was overwhelming. It was as though these things were right in my bedroom. In my mind's eye I saw the side of a horse and a portion of a leather saddle. I couldn't have been more than a few inches from them. My vision was strange, it was as though I were looking through a pipe. I only saw what was directly in front of me, no peripheral vision at all. Slowly I started to look down at what I suppose were my feet. I was wearing black boots which were covered with a dry film of dirt. The ground around my feet was dusty dirt with little patches of scrub grass. I stared at my boots and the dirt for a long time. I began to feel how sweaty my feet were inside these boots and I didn't like it. Suddenly I heard someone behind me. They were calling me, but they were calling me 'Lexington.' Somehow I knew this was my name in this place so I turned around to see who was calling. As I looked at the man I knew he was my brother, Tim. He didn't look like Tim but I knew it was he. He said for me to come over where he was and get something to eat before we had to ride on. It was as though I was drugged. It was very hard to walk but I managed to move over toward him and some other men sitting around a campfire. Like a slow-motion camera, my eyes took in everything though I didn't know what was going on. As I sat down to eat I began to smell the fire and the food. I still could smell horses, leather and sweat strongly but the smoke of the fire was strong and somehow familiar. I looked over at Tim and wondered if he'd noticed that I wasn't this guy Lexington.

But he just looked up at me and told me to hurry up and eat, it wasn't safe for us to linger around here too long. Since I couldn't see except for what was directly in front of me, I began to worry that I wouldn't be able to find the food and eat. Somehow my hands found the food and I slowly ate. Then I suddenly realized that this was a past life, that I had actually lived this life with my present brother Tim. During this realization I had the feeling my mother was behind me and I turned to see her. She was going to introduce me to some of her friends. I was afraid she was going to ask me to tell them my name and I didn't know it. But she turned to her friends and said, 'This is my son, Lexington.' I was dumbfounded. I just looked at her, dressed in the clothes of Early American settlers, and wondered what this was all about. Then just as suddenly I saw a map of North America. A dark, bold line began to move across the map and I knew it was showing me where I had traveled during this life-time. Then when the line stopped moving I knew it was where I died and I became uncomfortable because the death experience was coming back to me. The scene was once again around the campfire with my brother and the other men. Tim looked up at me and I knew he loved me and knew what was about to happen and didn't want me to die. I heard a rustling noise in the bushes to my left side but since my vision could only see directly in front of me I couldn't see who was coming. I felt a powerful blow to my head and as I started to lose consciousness I looked over at Tim who was shooting his gun as fast as he could and yelling, 'No, No! Don't die Lex! Don't die!' Somehow I knew we'd be together again but it was over for now, nothing could be done to keep me alive. My face was lying in the dusty dirt and I just stayed there, looking at the dirt, feeling my breath move in and out of my nostrils, and thinking about life. I felt sorry for Tim. I didn't want him to be left without me and I didn't want him to be so hurt. Somehow I felt I had always been a burden to him. I was never tough enough or smart enough for this wild, untamed country. I thought to myself, 'I'll make this up to him. I'll make sure the next time we're together I stay with him through the entire life, never leaving him.' Then I heard a whirring sound in my ears and I knew I was leaving this life. It was this noise that woke me."

In the present life this dreamer had a younger brother called Tim, and he was very protective of him. The two of them went everywhere together. However, the man who dreamed this dream was getting married in a week and was planning to move away from his younger brother to live in his wife's hometown. After having the dream, he asked his younger brother to transfer to a college in his wife's hometown. Tim did and the two of them continue to be very close.

Most past life dreams reveal fragments of a past life. Usually the fragment is an image, smell or sound that has left a lasting impression on the soul's mind. For example, a college professor frequently awoke from a nightmare in which he was choking on sand. The dreams were so real that he would actually be choking when he awoke. This professor was a white man who specialized in Black Studies. He had always found Black Culture and History to be of great interest to him. One day he was listening to a lecture by Alex Haley in which Mr. Haley told of how the Africans who were kidnapped and taken aboard the slave ships would commit suicide by deliberately swallowing sand from the beach. The professor was stunned. He knew immediately what his dream was about. He was recalling the most powerful image in his mind as he committed suicide on the beaches of Africa in a previous life. A traumatic death experience from a past life is often recalled because of the profound impression it leaves on the soul's mind. Such was the case with this professor, the image and sensation staying with him in the form of a recurring dream.

Again, the only way we can distinguish between a true past life recall and an imagined one is to objectively see how well it fits with our present nature and life. In the case of the professor, his present interests and work supported the dream and the subsequent realization that he had lived a past life as a black African man who had committed suicide by swallowing sand.

Self-Realization

I'm using the term self-realization as a catch-all for intuitive perceptions, deja vu, spontaneous revelations, repetitive mental images, "gut feelings" and all the other forms of personal insight into one's deeper memories. If we open up to the possibility of reincarnation, we will begin to see many indications of our soul's past. Our natural talents, our taste in food, clothing and stories, our innate characteristics, our primary interests all indicate our soul's past experiences. When we open to the possibility of reincarnation, we begin to allow ourselves to see and feel the memories of our soul. Here's an example.

A young man was working at a printing and mailing company as a zip code sorter. It 's a very non-mechanical job, requiring that one simply sort the mail by zip code. One Friday afternoon two of the printing press operators quit their jobs, leaving the company in a terrible bind. The zip code sorter asked the manager if he could come in the next day and work with one of the remaining printers to learn how to operate the presses. This was a ridiculous request because printing required a great deal of technical training and apprenticeship before someone could correctly operate a press. But because the circumstances were so unusual, the manager gave his permission. This young man quickly became one of the best printers the company had ever had. He said that it was all very natural for him. The smell of the ink was so familiar to him that he just felt wonderful being around it. The machines were so quickly understood by him, that he felt he had operated them before. And the process of printing was also easily grasped by him. He went on to become the supervisor and eventually the manager of the entire operation.

On a visit to Williamsburg, Virginia he happened to walk into the old colonial printer's shoppe that had been restored to its original form. Without any warning, he began to feel very strange. The smell of the wood, the ink and the sounds of the wooden press came rushing at him with such intensity he left the building. After sitting outside for several minutes, he got up and went back inside the restored print shoppe. Slowly he walked through it, knowing that he had worked there in a previous life in Colonial America. He watched how the other people looked around and commented on the different items in the shop, and a deep sense of life's true breadth came upon him. He was never quite the same again. He had gained a new sense of the continuity of Life, and gained it in a very personal way. It was no longer an intellectual concept for him; he knew it first-hand, in his being.

CHAPTER SIX
STARTING WHERE YOU ARE:
**A Practical Approach Toward
Working with Your Present Life
and Relationships**

One of the problems with knowing about reincarnation and its influence on our lives is that we tend to live with one eye looking into the past, always searching for insights into who was who and what was the past cause of some present problem or opportunity. I am not saying that this is necessarily bad. In fact, it is well for us to know "from whence we came as well as whither we goeth!" But too often we forget to make the most of our present life and relationships, to take hold of what lies before us and build a better present and future.

I think this backward looking attitude is at the root of some of the problems of countries who believe in reincarnation. Though they have a deep sense of life's true expanse and purposes, they have too readily submitted to the cycles of reincarnation and the forces of karma, allowing themselves to be carried along on the currents of life and the Universal Law of

Cause and Effect. Whereas, even though the West has lost its understanding of the broader life in which reincarnation is a reality, it has developed a powerful sense of self-determination, taking hold of free will and using it to its greatest potential. The present and the future have become the primary arena of activity for the West, with some very good results. Unfortunately, in most Western societies the will is mostly used in the pursuit of material accomplishment rather than spiritual.

I believe blending these two approaches to life is the best answer. *Now* is the best time, the best place and the best chance for achieving spiritual awakening and enlightenment; the rest of soul life, particularly the past, does add to our understanding of the whole picture and gives us insights into how best to use our present opportunities and limitations.

Since it is the twin gifts of free will and individual consciousness that gave us life, eternal life, and eventually led to our spiritual downfall, then it is free will and individual consciousness that will lead us to our spiritual reawakening and the achievement of our ultimate fulfillment and happiness. If you recall from Chapter One, the reason for our fall from original grace was our heightened focus on our own desires to the exclusion of others and the Whole, and the subsequent use of our free will to get our way despite the will of others and the Whole. In this way, we began to conceive of ourselves as separate from the Whole and the others around us. We lost a sense of just how our actions, words and thoughts affected the rest of life, thus we naturally came into direct conflict with the Law of Cause and Effect. Now, if we take hold of ourselves and make our wills one with the Law, in harmony again with the will of the Universal Consciousness or God, as we have come to call It, then we will rise again to our former place among the wonders of Life; true fulfill-ment, peace and lasting happiness will be ours. How-ever, this is not going to be achieved quickly or easily. Perhaps this is why Jesus said, "In patience, possess ye your souls." Much has happened, and it will not all be changed without effort and time.

So, let's begin where we are, with the personal charac-teristics we presently possess and the people around us now and the life situation we are currently facing.

First, we must establish our ideal, our standard by which to measure ourselves and our progress. Without a standard, we won't even know what an ideal, spiri-tually attuned person is like, nor can we apply our-selves toward its realization. We need an ideal, a stan-dard by which we can become the soul we were meant to be from the beginning. This is done through emu-lating the Ideal, assimilating Its nature into our own until we and the Ideal are one.

Determining our Ideal is difficult, but it is also very natural for us. As children, each of us had and used an Ideal (or ideals; there may be several) to guide our growth. Someone around us or some image of what was an ideal man or woman was before us, and our little child-minds, so pliant and impressionable, took firm hold upon this image and internalized it. As adults, however, we need another Ideal, a spiritual one. And, whereas the ideal held as a child may not have been conscious, it is with *conscious* awareness that we must choose our Ideal. Who we choose or what collec-tive image of the ideal, spiritually awakened individual we claim will certainly depend a great deal upon our own individual background. Our native culture, religion, race and our childhood experiences are going to influence our choice of an Ideal. A person who was born and raised in the Far East would certainly find Buddha or Krishna a more natural spiritual Ideal than Abraham or Moses. And a Near Eastern person would probably find Mohammed a more natural spiritual Ideal than Jesus of Nazareth. Nevertheless, there is only one God, only one Whole, only one Universal Consciousness. There may be many prophets and saints from many different cultures, and religions with many different ideas about what is best for enlightenment; but since there is only one God, there is ultimately only One to Whom we will all be attuned. In the end, it is the same God from whom all of us have descended that we will eventually ascend to again. Therefore, I suggest we remain open to the many ways in which humanity has experienced God, learning from each. Ultimately, of course, we have to take hold of that one with whom we can identify and set it as our own standard, our Ideal.

For example, if I set Jesus Christ as my Ideal, accepting that He is the Way, the Truth and the Light, then I provide myself with a standard to live by and to aspire to. I would attempt to love others, even my enemies. I would strive not to judge or condemn anyone. I would seek God with all my heart, mind, body and soul, and love my neighbors as myself. In other words, I would try to *live* by His guidelines with the assumption that these guidelines would bring me closer to my heavenly, spiritual nature and understanding. But an Ideal is more than this. I would also try to *be* like Christ. In His words, "You must eat my flesh and drink my blood." I must so assimilate His consciousness and will that I come to truly know Him first hand. In Christ's teachings, Jesus has gone to the Father and by so doing He was able to send the Holy Spirit to abide with us, comfort us and show us all things. Therefore, I must receive the Holy Spirit. This, of course, is not going to be a normal everyday experience! But Christ's teachings were, on the whole, very practical and relevant to daily life. So, it's not that I will separate myself from others or my life, but will simply approach others and my life with an attunement to my Ideal, a sense of how a spiritually attuned person reacts to situations and people.

Second, one of the best things we can do is set a direction for ourselves. Decide what it is we want most — how we would like our relationships to be, what kind of person we would like to be, and what we would like to be doing with our life and the lives of others. In other words, we need to identify our goals and prioritize them. Of course, our Ideal will influence the goals we select. But we shouldn't let all of this get too spacey or lofty. Spiritual growth and goals need to be very practical and relevant to our lives; otherwise we again begin to waste the opportunities before us. Here is the best place, these are the best people, and this is the best time to begin. Beyond our present circumstances are dreams, but within these circumstances are the steps toward living those dreams.

With our goals in mind, we will begin to make every choice that comes before us according to how it contributes to or distracts from our Ideal. We will no longer let the circumstances of life bat us around, pushing us in whatever direction it goes.

However, before we get too far along with setting goals, it is well for us to determine just *why* we want certain goals. What motivates us to seek these goals? It is very important that we know *why* we are seeking something as well as what it is we are seeking, because deep within the "why" is hidden the eventual reward. Happiness and fulfillment are more a result of "why we do" than "what we do." This is how two individuals who have equally the same opportunities and limitations in life can be so different in their happiness and sense of fulfillment. If we seek goals for weak or even wrong reasons, we will be disappointed when we reach them. Therefore, knowing why we are seeking a specific goal is as important as knowing what goal we are seeking.

1) What is our direction and goal? and 2) Why is it our direction and goal? With these two questions fairly well sketched-out in our heads and hearts, and our Ideal ever reflecting our ultimate image, we can begin to live our lives like never before. When life's rocky road takes a turn for the worse, we can view the situation or the relationship from the perspective of our goal, ask why it is our goal, how our Ideal would act in this situation, and then proceed to make the best decision we can and keep going toward our goal. Only in this way will our life ever reach its fullest potential and our ultimate future open up before us. Only in this way will we regain control over our destiny, fate and karma.

This goal-oriented life is not some grand crusade to a distant paradise. It is as practical and near as the very next person that walks up to us and our decision how to act and react. It's today, as we sit down and begin to write out a plan, select our Ideal, our goals and a direction. It's the next purchase we make, the next letter we write, the next activity we choose to do during our off-hours. In these little, everyday decisions lie the building blocks of a new you and me, and a new life.

THE ROLE OF SUFFERING

Rarely does life yield its fruits or do we gain in understanding and growth without some pain and suffering. As athletes are fond of saying, "No pain, no gain." No matter how high our ideals, how noble our goal, how loving our heart, we will experience hardships, disappointments, stumbling-blocks and, occasionally deep, painful sorrow along the way. I wish it could be different, but it simply is not. Suffering plays a role in transformation and growth. It is not a sign of failure, or that God has deserted us, or an indication that we have sinned in previous lives and therefore must suffer the consequences.

Of course, I wouldn't go looking for suffering. In fact, I'd suggest we approach our spiritual journey with enthusiasm, expectancy and joy, and look upon suffering as the ashes of the Phoenix, from which we will rise up and take hold of life like never before!

Also, fear, excuses and submission are stumbling-blocks to growth and transformation that each of us experiences. We simply must try our best to shake them off and move ahead with hope and expectancy. It is better for us to make a wrong decision and learn from it, than to make no decision. Fear, excuses and submission must be met with courage, forthrightness and willpower. If we can learn to forgive ourselves, understand our human and divine natures and remain devoted to our Ideal and goals, we will awaken to our higher selves and the vast expanse of spiritual life.

I know a woman who had been married more than 20 years. One day while she was humming along in her happy home, her husband came up to her and told her he was no longer in love with her and had found another woman with whom he wanted to live. It was the ultimate defeat for her; she was completely destroyed. The man to whom she had contributed so much, sacrificing and giving when it hurt, was now leaving as though nothing had passed between them. The home she painstakingly built over the years was coming down all around her. And it got worse. Eventually, she had to go out of her beautiful home life and work among aggressive, fast-paced achievers, who looked upon her as they would a defective part. Her world was turned upside down, crashing in on her. She spent many painful nights crying alone, no one to care or comfort her. It all seemed so senseless and unfair, without any ultimate purpose to it. She came very close to falling off the edge of life into an abyss of hopelessness that many of us have caught a glimpse of in our own lives. However, the days turned into months, the months into years and though many were the times she came close to quitting, she never did. Every time she was downed by the overwhelming impact of the whole affair, she managed to get back up again and go on a little farther until one day she realized it really didn't hurt anymore. In fact, like never before in her life, it seemed she held the destiny of her life in her own hands. She was strong, resilient, and deeply self-assured. Nothing could destroy her. She had experienced a devastating loss and yet lived to tell about it, even with some humor. And despite all of this, she retained her love of the home and home life. In fact, she remarried at 48 and this marriage turned out to be so much more mutually fulfilling and nourishing than the former marriage that she now doesn't know how she endured the first one! Many more people are involved in her life now than ever before. Life is richer and more vital than it had been before. But it honestly was impossible to see this end during those early periods of shock and suffering.

There were some very important elements involved in her successful transformation and resurrection. First of all, this woman had enough self-esteem to sustain her sense of self-worth even though she was surrounded with apparent failure and totally inadequate skills for living on her own. Secondly, her hopeful, positive attitude was stronger than the hopelessness and negativity that was surrounding her on every side. Thirdly, and most importantly, she did the best she could with what she had. She tried and tried and tried again, and like water on the stone, broke through the seemingly unbreakable barrier to a happy, fulfilling life, drop by drop, step by step, until it was done.

Now if we take this to a spiritual level and see how these few years of pain and suffering have affected her eternal soul and its destiny, we will see that she is much more capable now of surmounting any illusions and limitations that the world has placed on her spiritual consciousness. By overcoming the loss of the powerful paradigm within which she lived during her first marriage and coming to a new and greater vision of life beyond it, her inner self can more easily break out of the physical, material paradigm that it has so completely accepted as the only reality and rise to a new, grander life beyond it. This woman's soul will never be the same again. In any future incarnations she will retain her newfound strength and wisdom, and will be able to apply it to any other limitations that she may be under.

With all of this in mind let's list these tools for attaining our ultimate happiness and fulfillment:

1) **SELECT OUR IDEAL.** By what standard are we willing to measure our progress? Who or what collection of characteristics represents the ideal, spiritually awakened individual for us? With our Ideal clearly established, we can proceed to live, act, think and make decisions in light of how our Ideal would do such. The more we assimilate the characteristics of our Ideal, the more closely we become the Ideal, until we and the Ideal are one in the same.

2) **SET A GOAL, A DIRECTION.** It should include how we want to be, how we want to be with others, what type of relationships we want, what type of life-style we want and what we most want to do with our energy, talent and life. The setting of our goals will be guided by our Ideal, our goals leading us closer to our Ideal.

3) **DETERMINE WHY WE SET A GOAL AND DIRECTION.** What motivates us to seek these goals? Why do we want to be a certain way? Why do we want to do certain things? Why do we want certain types of relationships? It's as important to know why as it is to know what, because the "why" reveals the purpose and

the ultimate end thereof.

4) **MAKE CHOICES ACCORDING TO HOW THEY CONTRIBUTE TO OR DISTRACT FROM THE ATTAINMENT OF OUR GOAL.** Within reason, let's not allow life's circumstances and other people to determine what our life is going to be like. No matter what happens, let's seek to keep ourselves on course toward our goal. Of course, this should be tempered with the awareness that spiritual growth dictates a loving concern for others and the Will of God. But within this aura of loving concern and responsiveness, we must try to also keep on our course.

5) **MAINTAIN OUR SELF-ESTEEM.** Our thoughts and feelings affect our mental and physical being, and attract similar reactions from others. Let's remember that old saying: "There is so much good in the worst of us and so much bad in the best of us that it doesn't pay for any of us to think poorly of the rest of us!" And it especially does not pay for us to think poorly of ourselves—there's simply too much good still within the worst of us. No sin is too great, no error too deadly that a merciful Creator and a repentant heart can't heal it. Each of us is vital to the Whole, so we must retain our self-esteem.

6) **USE WHAT WE HAVE IN HAND AND BEGIN WHERE WE ARE WITH WHOMEVER WE ARE PRESENTLY LIVING.** There is nothing beyond the present situation, circumstances and people in our lives that is going to help us get anywhere more than what is right before us. By taking hold of the present and using it

toward our goal and in accord with our Ideal, we make the most practical, positive move we can make. Begin here, now, not tomorrow or with some other person or job or opportunity, unless it becomes very clear that a change is the only way we will attain our goal. Looking beyond present abilities and limitations, and our present friends and relatives, and our present job or activity, is dreaming, not working toward a new life and a new level of awareness. That begins with what is at hand today, in little ways each day.

7) **KEEP A POSITIVE, HOPEFUL AND EXPECTANT ATTITUDE.** Fear, excuses and submission are the stumbling-blocks to transformation and growth. Let's not waste any energy or time with them. In the midst of hopelessness, struggle to remain hopeful and looking for that one little opportunity that will get us going in the chosen direction again.

8) **KNOW THAT SUFFERING IS A PART OF TRANS-FORMATION AND GROWTH.** Let's not go looking for it, but let's also not be discouraged or disappointed if our path begins to hurt. The cross surely must have been a bitter end for Jesus to accept after healing and teaching to so many about the joy of heaven and the true purpose of life. Yet, even as He asked why He had been forsaken by our Heavenly Father, He was being prepared for a glory that no one had known before, victory over death. Out of this pain rose a light, a truth and a way that mankind has acknowledged as divinely guided and that many now aspire to achieve and know in their own lives. So it is with the little sufferings we experience in our lives. From out of them come a resur-

rected you and me, changed forever, and better for having experienced it.

APPENDIX

EDGAR CAYCE

Edgar Cayce was born on a farm near Hopkinsville, Kentucky, on March 18, 1877. As a child he displayed unusual powers of perception. At the age of six he told his parents that he could see and talk with "visions," sometimes of relatives who had recently died. He could also sleep with his head on his schoolbooks and awake with a photographic memory of their contents. However, after completing seventh grade he left school to find his place in the world. When he was twenty-one, he developed a paralysis of the throat muscles which caused him to lose his voice. When doctors were unable to find a physical cause for this condition, Edgar Cayce asked a friend to help him re-enter the same kind of hypnotic sleep that had enabled him to memorize his schoolbooks as a child. His friend gave him the necessary suggestions, and once he was in this trance state, Edgar spoke clearly and directly to the problem. He recommended some specific medication and manipulative therapy which successfully restored his voice.

Doctors around Hopkinsville and Bowling Green, Kentucky, took advantage of Cayce's unique talent to diagnose their own patients. They soon discovered that all Cayce needed was the name and address of a patient and he could "tune in" telepathically to that individual's mind and body. The patient didn't have to be near Cayce, wherever they were he could tune-in to them.

When one of the young M.D.'s working with Cayce submitted a report on his strange abilities to a clinical research society in Boston, the reactions were amazing. On October 9, 1910, *The New York Times* carried two pages of headlines and pictures. From then on, people from all over the country sought the "sleeping prophet," as he was to become known.

His routine for conducting a trance-diagnosis was to recline on a couch, hands folded across his chest, and breathe deeply. Eventually, his eyelids would begin fluttering. This was the signal to the conductor (usually his wife, Gertrude) to close them and make verbal contact with Cayce's subconscious by giving a suggestion. Unless this procedure was timed to synchronize with his fluttering eyelids, Cayce would proceed beyond his trance state and simply fall fast asleep. Once the suggestion was made, Cayce would proceed to describe the patient as though they were sitting right next to him, his mind functioning much as an x-ray scanner seeing into every cell of their body. When he was finished, he would say, "Ready for questions." However, in many cases his mind would have already anticipated the patient's questions, answering them during the main session. Eventually, he would say, "We are through for the present," whereupon the conductor would give the suggestion to return to consciousness.

If this procedure was in any way violated, Cayce was in serious personal danger. On one occasion, he remained in a trance state for three days and had actually been given up for dead by the attending doctors.

At each session a stenographer (usually Gladys Davis Turner, his personal secretary) would record everything Cayce said. Sometimes during a trance session Cayce would even correct the stenographer's spelling. It was as though his mind was in touch with everything around him and beyond.

It was August 10, 1923 before anyone thought to ask the "sleeping" Cayce for insights beyond physical health, questions about life, death and human destiny. In a small hotel room in Dayton, Ohio, Arthur Lammers asked the first set of philosophical questions that were to lead to an entirely new way of using Cayce's strange abilities. It was during this line of questioning that Cayce first began to talk about reincarnation as though it were as real and natural as a physical body.

Eventually, Edgar Cayce, following advice from his own "readings," as they were now being called, moved to Virginia Beach, Virginia, and set up a hospital where he continued to conduct his "Physical Readings" for the health of others. But he also continued this new line of readings called "Life Readings." From 1925 through 1944 he conducted some 2500 of these Life Readings, describing the past lives of individuals as casually as if everyone understood reincarnation was a reality. Such subjects as deep-seated fears, mental blocks, vocational talents, innate urges and abilities, marriage difficulties, child training, etc., were examined in the light of what Edgar Cayce called the "karmic patterns" resulting from previous lives spent by the individual's soul on the earth plane.

When he died on January 3, 1945, in Virginia Beach, he left well over 14,000 documented stenographic records of the telepathic-clairvoyant readings he had given for more than 6,000 different people over a period of forty-three years.

The readings constitute one of the largest and most impressive records of psychic perception. Together with their relevant records, correspondence and reports, they have been cross-indexed under thousands of subject headings and placed at the disposal of psychologists, students, writers and investigators who still come to examine them. Of course, they are also available to the general public.

A foundation known as the A.R.E. (Association for Research and Enlightenment, Inc., 67th St. & Atlantic Avenue, Virginia Beach, VA 23451) was founded in 1932 to preserve these readings. As an open-membership research society, it continues to index and catalogue the information, initiate investigation and experiments, and conduct conferences, seminars and lectures. The A.R.E. also has the largest and finest library of parapsychological and metaphysical books in the world. It also maintains a mail-order bookstore with a catalog of over 300 titles of the best books in these areas of human study.

REINCARNATION & CHRISTIANITY

Reincarnation has had little, if any, place in mainstream Christianity. However, there is evidence that it was an accepted concept during the time of Christ, shortly after His resurrection, and even long before His birth. Furthermore, there is some evidence that the concepts of reincarnation were stricken from the Church theology and even modified in the Bible at the Fifth Ecumenical Congress of Constantinople in 553 A.D. At this Congress, the writings of the early church father, Origen, whose writings developed from the teachings of many earlier teachers, including Plato, were denounced and expunged from the Church's body of knowledge.

Here are a few examples of these early teachings.

> "Know that if you become worse you will go to the worse souls, and if better, to the better souls; and in every succession of life and death you will do and suffer what like must fitly suffer at the hands of like."
>
> PLATO (582-507 B.C.), *The Republic*

"Every soul...comes into this world strengthened by the victories or weakened by the defeats of its previous life. Its place in this world as a vessel appointed to honor or dishonor, is determined by its previous merits or demerits. Its work in this world determines its place in the world which is to follow this."

ORIGEN, *De Principiis*

"We were in being long before the foundation of the world; we existed in the eye of God, for it is our destiny to live in Him. We are reasonable creatures of the Divine Word; therefore we have existed from the beginning, for in the beginning was the Word."

St. Clement of Alexandria (150-220 A.D.)

"...it is absolutely necessary that the soul should be healed and purified, and if this does not take place during its life on earth, it must be accomplished in future lives."

St. Gregory (257-332 A.D.)

"The message of Plato, the purest and the most luminous of all philosophy, has at last scattered the darkness of error, and now shines forth mainly in Plotinus, a Platonist so like his master that one would think they lived together, or rather—since so long a period of time separates them—that Plato was born again in Plotinus."

St. Augustine (354-430 A.D.)

Beyond the teachings and ideas of these early church fathers, we actually find quotes from within the Bible which may indicate a knowledge and acceptance of reincarnation. Here are a few examples.

"The Lord possessed me in the beginning of his way, before his works of old.

"I was set up from everlasting, from the beginning, or ever the earth was.

"When there were no depths, I was brought forth; when there were no fountains abounding with water.

"Before the mountains were settled, before the hills was I brought forth:

"While as yet he had not made the earth, nor the fields, nor the highest part of the dust of the world.

"When he prepared the heavens, I was there: when he set a compass upon the face of the depth:

"When he established the clouds above: when he strengthened the fountains of the deep:

"When he gave to the sea his decree, that the waters should not pass his commandment: when he appointed the fountains of the earth:

"Then I was by him, as one brought up with him..."

PROVERBS 8:22-30

"Behold, I will send you Elijah the prophet, before the coming of the great and dreadful day of the Lord."

MALACHI 4:5

"And His disciples asked Him, saying, 'Why then say the scribes that Elias (Elijah) must first come?' And Jesus answered and said unto them, 'Elias truly shall first come, and restore all things. But I say unto you that Elias is come already, and they knew him not, but have done unto him whatsoever they listed. Likewise shall also the Son of Man suffer of them.' Then the disciples understood that he spake unto them of John the Baptist."

MATTHEW 17:9-13

"...all the prophets and the law prophesied until John (the Baptist). And if ye will receive it, this is Elias, which was to come. He that hath ears to hear, let him hear."

MATTHEW 11:13, 14

"And as Jesus passed by, he saw a man which was blind from his birth. And His disciples asked Him, saying, 'Master, who did sin, this man or his parents; that he was born blind?'"

JOHN 9:1,2

"Him that overcometh will I make a pillar in the temple of the Lord, and he shall go no more out."

REVELATION 3:12

Certainly reincarnation is not accepted as a teaching of Modern Christianity, but there is evidence it was at one time as well understood by Christians as by Hindus and Buddhists.

BOOKS FOR FURTHER STUDY

HYPNOSIS, REVERIES & GUIDED IMAGERY

I find it very difficult to recommend books on these subjects. It's a quickly changing field, with new insights and techniques coming almost as fast as new computers! And yet, the principles upon which the entire field of study is based, have not changed much. Therefore, we really need to read two separate types of books; those on the basic principles and those on the latest techniques. Here are my recommendations:

The Laws of Psychic Phenomena, Thomson Jay Hudson; Hudson-Cohan Publishing Co., 1925.

This book is a must; upon its principles are based the entire structure of the inner realms of consciousness and how they operate.

Mind Probe, Irene Hickman
Hickman Systems, 1983.

This is also an excellent book for gaining an understanding of how our inner consciousness may be approached.

Self-Hypnosis: Creating Your Own Destiny, Henry Bolduc; A.R.E. Press, 1985.

Here are the tools for getting yourself started on your venture inward.

Psychosynthesis, Robert Assagioli
Viking Press, 1973.

This is a much more involved approach to the subject than perhaps most of us would like to attempt, but it is one of the principal books of this field.

Venture Inward, Hugh Lynn Cayce
Harper & Row, 1964.

The son of the late Edgar Cayce and the long-time president and chairman of the Association for Research and Enlightenment has put together a broad overview of the venture into "inner space" consciousness.

PAST LIFE MEMORY & REINCARNATION CONCEPTS

These books contain some of the best insights into how reincarnation affects us and how some of us have remembered our past lives.

Many Mansions, Gina Cerminara
Signet, 1967 The New American Library

Absolutely filled with examples of karma and past lives from the Edgar Cayce readings.

Edgar Cayce on Reincarnation, Noel Langley
Warner Books, 1967

This book contains many of the past-life readings given by Edgar Cayce. It also has a large section on how reincarnation and Christianity parted company.

Born Again, Hans Holzer
Doubleday, 1970

Many examples of how Holzer gained past-life memories from hypnotic subjects, with many past-life stories.

Past-Life Therapy, Dick Sutphen
Valley of the Sun, 1983

Dick Sutphen is one of the main figures in the field of reincarnation. Using hypnotic age-regression, he explores the inner consciousness and past-life memories of several individuals.

Stay in Touch
and Informed

If you would like to receive periodic updates on the latest books and tapes from Inner Vision Publishing Co., fill in the form below and mail it to:

Inner Vision Publishing Co.
Box 1117, Seapines Station
Virginia Beach, VA 23451

Or Call Toll-Free:

1-800-227-0172
in Virginia call, 1-804-671-1777

Other Books & Tapes
from INNER VISION

BOOKS --

☐ BORN AGAIN & AGAIN: How Reincarnation Occurs, $8.95
by John Van Auken

☐ PAST LIVES & PRESENT RELATIONSHIPS, $8.95
by John Van Auken

☐ GETTING HELP FROM YOUR DREAMS, $9.95
by Henry Reed

☐ DREAM QUEST WORKBOOK, $16.95
by Henry Reed

☐ THE INNER POWER OF SILENCE: A Universal Way
of Meditation, Mark Thurston, $7.95

☐ FATIMA PROPHECY, $9.95
by Ray Stanford

☐ THE SPIRIT UNTO THE CHURCHES (Spiritual Centers
of the Human Body), Ray Stanford, $12.95

CASSETTE TAPES --

☐ TIPS ON MEDITATION (2 Sides)
by John Van Auken, $6.95

☐ PAST LIVES & PRESENT RELATIONSHIPS (2-Tape Set),
by John Van Auken, $14.95

☐ ADDICTIONS: New Ideas for Understanding and
Overcoming Them, (2 Sides) by Henry Reed, $9.95

Call Toll-Free:
1-800-227-0172
in Virginia call, 1-804-671-1777

INNER VISION PUBLISHING CO.
Box 1117, Seapines Station
Virginia Beach, VA 23451

Please send me the books and tapes I have checked. I enclosed a check or
money order for the full amount. I understand that INNER VISION pays all
postage and handling costs. (Allow 4 weeks for delivery.)

☐ **Please Send Me Your Free Catalog.**

Name _____

Address _____

City _____

State _____ Zip _____